Leather Crafting

in an afternoon®

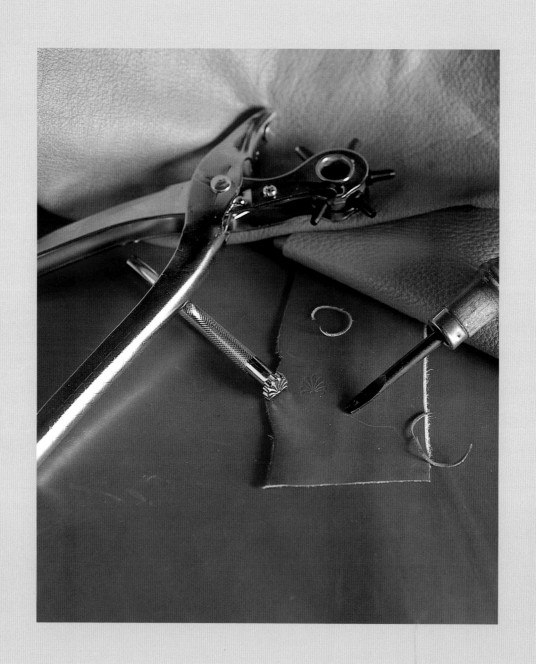

Leather Crafting

in an afternoon®

Mickey Baskett

Sterling Publishing Co., Inc.
New York

Prolific Impressions Production Staff:

Editor in Chief: Mickey Baskett
Copy Editor: Phyllis Mueller
Graphics: Dianne Miller, Karen Turpin
Styling: Kirsten Jones
Photography: Jerry Mucklow, Joel Tressler
Administration: Jim Baskett

Library of Congress Cataloging-in-Publication Data

Baskett, Mickey.
  Leather crafting in an afternoon / Mickey Baskett.
    p. cm.
  Includes index.
  ISBN 1-4027-0337-6
  1. Leatherwork. I. Title.
TT290 .B35 2004
475.53'1--dc22

2003017384

10 9 8 7 6 5 4 3 2 1

Published in paperback in 2006 by Sterling Publishing Co., Inc.
387 Park Avenue South, New York, N.Y. 10016
© 2003 by Prolific Impressions, Inc.
Produced by Prolific Impressions, Inc.
160 South Candler St., Decatur, GA 30030
Distributed in Canada by Sterling Publishing
c/o Canadian Manda Group, 165 Dufferin Street,
Toronto, Ontario, Canada M6K 3H6
Distributed in the United Kingdom by GMC Distribution Services,
Castle Place, 166 High Street, Lewes, East Sussex, England BN7 1XU
Distributed in Australia by Capricorn Link (Australia) Pty. Ltd.
P.O. Box 704, Windsor, NSW 2756 Australia
Printed in China

Sterling ISBN-13: 978-1-4027-0337-9 Hardcover
        ISBN-10 1-4027-0337-6

        ISBN-13: 978-1-4027-4059-6 Paperback
        ISBN-10: 1-4027-4059-X

For information about custom editions, special sales, premium
and corporate purchases, please contact Sterling Special Sales
Department at 800-805-5489 or specialsales@sterlingpub.com.

Acknowledgements

A special thank you to the following companies for supplying products to create the projects in this book.

All of the leather and suede hides as well as tooling leather, and leather crafting tools were provided by: The Leather Factory, Inc., P.O. Box 50429, Fort Worth, TX 76105, 800-433-3201, www.leatherfactory.com

A very good cement for leather is from Fiebing Co., Inc. Milwaukee, WI 53204, 800-558-1033, www.fiebing.com

Products for painting and stamping on leather such as FolkArt® Acrylic Paints, Outdoor Sealer, All Night Media rubber stamps, and inkpads were provided by: Plaid Enterprises, Inc., 3225 Westech Dr., Norcross, GA, 30092, 800-842-4197, www.plaidonline.com

Beaded fringe looks great on leather. The fringe used in this book was provided by: Expo International, Inc., 5631 Braxton Dr., Houston, TX 77036, 800-542-4367

The beautiful beads used to create the beading projects shown were from: Blue Moon Beads, Elizabeth Ward & Company, Inc., 4218 Howard Ave., Kensington, MD 20895, 800-377-6715, www.bluemoonbeads.com

When sewing leather a glover's needle is best to use. It is available from: Prym-Dritz® Corporation, Spartanburg, SC 29304, www.dritz.com

CONTENTS

Introduction

page 6

Supplies

Leather, Cutting Tools, Coloring Agents, Hole-making Tools,
Sewing Supplies & Adhesives

page 8 -13

Leather Crafting Skills

Cutting Leather, Finishing Edges, Hand Sewing,
Rubber Stamping, Tooling, Setting Metal Hardware

page 14 - 19

Leather Projects

Home Decor, Jewelry, Tabletop & Desk Accessories,
Journals, Purses & Totes

page 20 - 126

Leather is the perfect material for creating luxuries for yourself and your home. Leather is durable and resistant to weather. It can be shaped, cut, dyed, decorated with stamping or paint, tooled, and carved. It can even be sewn with a sewing machine. When cut, leather doesn't fray, which expands its possible applications for all types of projects. And – here's the best part – the more you use leather, the better it feels.

As with any art or craft, there are levels of involvement. You can choose to do a few quick and easy projects – or make your new pursuit a life's obsession. This book is meant to tantalize, entice, and introduce you to leather crafting, in hopes that the projects will intrigue you and be your springboard for delving deeper into this craft and becoming proficient in some of the many techniques introduced here.

The projects in this book cover a wide range of techniques. They are easy to accomplish, yet each could be explored, pursued, and embraced as a separate craft. As you become acquainted with a technique, you will realize how much more about it there is to learn. For example, this book introduces

At a leather crafting show, popular home decor items were lamps. This lampshade is made from rawhide and lacing on an antler base.

leather tooling with two very simple, lovely projects – a tooled rose trivet and a tooled bookmark. The projects can be done with a basic set of seven tools. Should you become intrigued with leather tooling, you'll find there are hundreds of tools available and nuances to the technique that experts debate regularly.

Layers of thin leather are laced together on a metal frame to make this beautiful lampshade.

As I researched leather crafting for this book, I was amazed to discover that from the east coast to the west coast and everywhere in-between there are clubs, guilds, shows, suppliers, and artisans involved in this craft. I attended several leather shows and even went way out west to Scottsdale, Arizona's Festival of the West. I was in awe of the saddle and tack makers who carve and tool thick leather with elegant designs. Other artisans made wallets, pouches, purses, boots, lampshades, and furniture. I was so tempted to come home with a

At a leather crafting show I decided you couldn't have too much leather. I enjoyed rummaging through piles of supple skins to choose the hides with just the right coloration for my project needs.

truckload of hides, and decided you can't have too much leather!

If you enjoy using the web, visit the International Internet Leathercrafters Guild website (http://iigl.org) to learn about meetings, shows, books, artisans, and suppliers available to you. Or visit your bookstore, library, or crafts store to find out more about this fascinating, enjoyable craft.

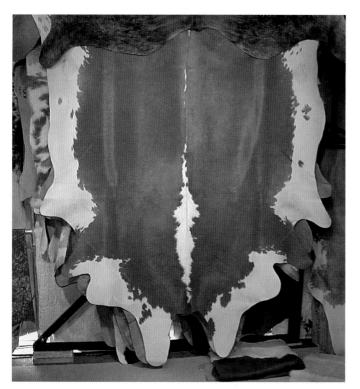

Larger hides are also available for larger projects.

SUPPLIES

Leather

Leather is an extremely supple and adaptable material to use for crafting. It can be cut with a variety of tools and sewn by machine or hand. It can be decorated with painting, tooling, stamping, beading, or by setting metal decorations and hardware. Not only can it be manipulated in a number of ways, but it is very durable – it lasts for years and can be used to make items that get lots of wear and tear, like furniture and shoes. Leather's versatility is astounding – it can be used to accomplish intricate jewelry pieces, sewn into soft and appealing pillows or purses, or hand craft shoes and furniture.

The animal skins you will use for crafting are called "tanned" leather. The skins of animals such as cows, sheep, deer, and goats have been processed by first removing the hair and epidermis, then by exposing the material to a chemical or natural vegetable bath. Tanning gives leather the characteristics we love – flexibility, strength, durability, and stretchability.

Leather has many grades, colors, textures, and weights. Leather thicknesses are expressed in ounces – the weight of the leather per square foot – so 1-2 oz. leather is very thin; 10-12 oz. leather is very thick. You can purchase leather as complete hides, small skins, or even small crafting pieces.

Familiarizing yourself with the various types of leather will allow you to choose the most appropriate leather for a particular job. Search through catalogs, online sellers, fabric stores, leather crafting supplies, and even shoe repair shops to see what is available to you.

Here are descriptions of some leather types that are appropriate for the type of projects and techniques in this book:
- **Garment & Upholstery Leather:** This grade of leather can be found in weights from 1-5 oz. The thinner weights are best for machine sewing.
- **Suede:** Suede is usually available in thinner weights such as 2-3 oz. It is appropriate for clothing, purses, pillows, or other projects that need a soft, fabric-like material. It is not appropriate for tooling.
- **Tooling Leather:** To be able to tool and carve leather, you will

need vegetable tanned leather that is not dyed. Calfskin or cowhide leather in 3-4 oz. weight is an excellent thickness for tooling.
- **Chamois Leather:** This machine-washable leather is great for making potholders, gloves, and clothing items.
- **Lacing or Thonging:** These are string-like strips of leather or suede that are available in many colors. It can be used to sew or "lace" pieces of leather together or to add decoration on leather edges.

WORK SURFACES

There are several types of surfaces you will need when working with leather. What you use depends upon the technique you are performing.
- **Cutting Mat:** A poly, self-healing mat with grid markings makes cutting easier when using a rotary cutter or utility knife.
- **Wooden Cutting Board:** This is a good general purpose surface for a variety of tasks, but for stamping and tooling leather, a wooden surface usually has too much "bounce" to be effective.
- **Stone Slab:** A 1-1/2" to 2" thick piece of marble or granite is the preferred surface for tooling leather. The thicker the piece, the better impression your tool will make.

Cutting Tools

Leather is easily cut. Choose quality, heavy-duty tools to make your job easier.

- **Scissors** can cut thin suedes and garment leather not heavier than 3-4 oz.

- **Leather Shears** are needed for heavier leathers.

- A **Rotary Cutter** is convenient for cutting thin leather for pattern pieces, for straight cuts on thinner leathers, or for cutting fringe.

- A **Utility Knife** or **Craft Knife** is needed for leathers heavier than 8 oz.

- A **Straight Edge**, such as a metal-edged ruler with a cork back, is useful for marking leather as well as for cutting when using a rotary cutter of utility knife.

- A **Swivel Knife** is used only for carving and tooling leather. Most knives have interchangeable small and large blades.

- An **Edge Beveller** is used for dressing the edges of thick leather.

Pictured left to right: Revolving hole punch, swivel knife, rotary cutter, scissors, metal ruler with cork backing. Tools are arranged on a marked cutting mat.

Hole Making Tools

- **Hole Punch:** This revolving punch is appropriate for punching holes for lacing, snaps, and other hardware and for creating decorative designs. A hole punch is available in single tube varieties, but a revolving punch allows for more options in sizes of holes.

- **Hole Chisels:** These chisels are great for making evenly spaced holes when doing hand sewing or holes for lacing. They may be referred to by the number of holes they make at a time, e.g., 2-prong chisel or 3-prong chisel.

- **Awl:** This very handy tool can make holes for sewing or for snaps and other hardware.

Setting Tools

Setting tools are used for setting hardware such as snaps, spots, eyelets, rivets, and grommets. Usually you need various types, depending upon the hardware you are using. There are rivet setters, snap setters, grommet setters, spot setters, and eyelet setters.

You can purchase tool sets that are multi-purpose. Many times you can purchase a kit includes the hardware and the setter. Deciding what to purchase depends upon how much of a technique you anticipate doing; if you plan to do only a few projects, then purchasing a kit with a setter and the hardware is the most economical choice.

Pictured left to right: Edge beveller, 3-prong hole chisel, snap setter, snaps.

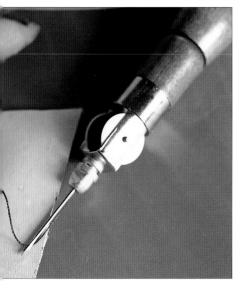

Hand sewing awl, above, & Woodburning Tool, below.

Sewing Supplies

- **Sewing Awls** are a must for hand sewing.
- **Thread** (waxed linen or nylon) is needed for hand sewing.
- A **Lacing Needle** is needed when using lacing or thonging.
- A **Stitching Pony** is a clamp that holds your work while you stitch.

Sewing Machine

Suede and leather that is thinner than 1/16" thick can easily be sewn on a sewing machine. Use sturdy poly-cotton thread and a leather needle and use a longer stitch length than you would for fabric. It's a good idea to consult your sewing machine manufacturer's manual for information on how to set the tension and to practice on a scrap piece of leather so you can test the tension and the stitch length before working on your actual project.

Use an awl or the tip of a bone folder to score sewing lines as guides for machine sewing on leather.

Woodburning Tool

Another way of decorating leather is by burning with a woodburning tool. This special tool looks like a small electric soldering iron with a fine tip. You must plug it into an electrical outlet and let it become hot. Use the burning tool as you would a pencil, drawing it directly on the grain side of the leather. You burn designs freehand or transfer a pattern and follow it. The hot tool will scorch the leather, and the harder you press, the darker the impression will be.

When used on leather, a woodburning tool may be referred to as a "branding tool."

Stamping Tools

Pictured at left from left to right: Tools and supplies for tooling – modeling tool with spoon modeler at one end and stylus at the other; an assortment of tooling stamps. Pictured at top is a poly mallet and a piece of granite, which can be used as a stamping surface.

Pictured below from top to bottom: Designs made with stamping tools, using the seeder, background, camouflage, pear shader, flourish design stamp, leaf design stamp, veiner, and beveller.

If you intend to model or carve leather – the process called "tooling", you will need stamping tools plus a few other items. A basic tool set is a good introduction for beginners.

- A **Mallet** is used to hit the end of the tool so that an impression is pressed into the leather. Mallets are made of poly material, rawhide, wood, or metal.

- A **Modeling Tool** is used to shape and form the leather.

- A **Stylus** is a handy tool for marking patterns on leather.

- The **Beveller** is used to shape the leather and produce a raised effect.

- A **Background Stamp** is used to add texture to the background. It looks like a series of nail pricks.

- The **Camouflage Tool** is used to give additional texture or to touch up areas. It can also be used for edging designs.

- The **Seeder** creates small circles for design work, such as flower centers, borders, etc.

- **Shaders** are used to shade and emboss areas.

- **Design Stamps** can be found in a variety of sizes and shapes, such as leaves, flowers, animals, etc.

Coloring Agents

Leather Dye: Dyes can be water-based or spirit-based. Dyes penetrate the leather so they do not obscure the grain of the material. They can be used to color the edges of the leather pieces or the surface. Large areas can be dyed using a brush or a sponge; small designs can be dyed by painting the dye with artist's paint brushes.

Acrylic Paints: These craft paints can be used on leather; however, because they are opaque they sit on the surface and obscure the grain. They are permanent and can add interesting surface decoration.

Rubber Stamps and Ink: Found in a wide variety of designs, rubber stamps add decorative details to leather. Ink pads come in a variety of colors. Acrylic craft paints also can be used with rubber stamps.

Acrylic craft paint, leather dye, artist brushes.

Below: Leather finish and adhesives.

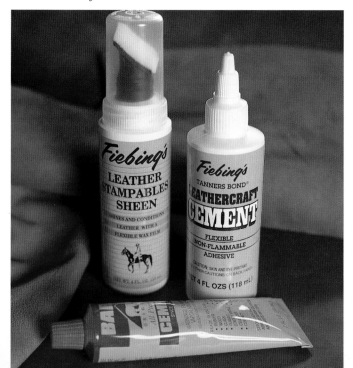

Leather Finishes

When you have tooled, dyed, stamped, or painted your leather you will want to give it a waterproof, protective coat of finish. You can also protect undyed (usually tooled) leather with a finish to keep it from getting dirty or greasy. Pre-dyed leather usually has already been protected with a finish.

Adhesives

Contact cement or leather cement is the best type of glue to use to bond two pieces of leather together. You can use **rubber cement** for tacking pieces together, but it will not form a permanent bond. Individual project instructions specify the type of glue to use.

LEATHER CRAFTING SKILLS

Cutting Leather

Thin leathers can be easily cut with **scissors** or **leather shears**. A **rotary cutter** is excellent for cutting thin leathers. It is especially helpful when cutting pattern pieces. Use a **cutting mat** when using the rotary cutter.

Cutting leather on a cutting mat using a rotary cutter.

Using a rotary tool for cutting fringe makes the job quick and easy.

Finishing Edges

To finish and round off the edges of thick (usually over 4 oz. weight) leather pieces and remove the sharp angles, use an **edge beveller**. To use, place the leather piece on a hard surface such as a stone slab, cutting mat, or wood cutting board. Hold the tool at a 45-degree angle as you push it along the edge. It will shave off the leather. This does not have to be done in one continuous strip – stopping and starting is okay. Dampening the edge helps when beveling very dry leather.

When beveling is complete, dye the edge to match the leather.

For a nice finished edge on thick pieces of leather, use the edge beveller tool to shave off a sharp edge.

Use leather dye of the same color as leather to dye the edges.

Hand Sewing

When sewing thick leather, holes for the stitching need to be marked and punched into the leather. For hand sewing, you will need: nylon or waxed linen thread, a clamp called a stitching pony, a sewing awl with needles, and a hole spacer, a hole chisel, or an awl. Start by marking a line on the leather where stitches are to be placed. *Tip:* Placing masking tape along back of leather is a great way to mark straight lines.

An awl can be used to punch one hole at a time into the leather, or a multi-hole chisel can be used to punch a series of holes. Once the holes are marked or punched, clamp the piece in a stitching pony.

Various types of stitches can be used for hand sewing: whipstitches, saddle stitches, back stitches, lacing stitches. Backstitching is done with one needle; saddle stitching is done with two needles.

Using a 3-prong hole chisel to make holes for stitching.

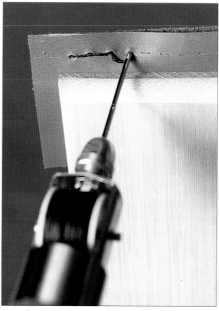

Stitching with an awl. The leather is clamped in a stitching pony.

Rubber Stamping

Beautiful decorative motifs can be added to leather with rubber stamping. Use permanent ink and stamp the design of your choice. When design is dry, coat with a waterproof leather finish.

Stamping leather with permanent ink.

Applying leather finish.

Tooling Leather

This very old technique has many devotees, and each has his or her own way of doing this craft. I have learned that with practice comes skill, and that many expert carvers and toolers have a sequence in which they use the various tools. One British practice is to use the tools in this order: beveller, pear shader, camouflage, veiner, seeder, background. I have found this to be a good way to come up with my own style – practice using the tools, read about what other toolers recommend, and try some techniques of my own.

YOU WILL NEED

Tooling leather (3-4 oz. weight is a good thickness to use)

Stylus

Sponge

Surface, such as a stone slab or wooden cutting board

Swivel knife

Stamping tools (modeling, pear shader, beveller, camouflage, seeder, veiner, background)

STEPS TO FOLLOW

Wet the Leather: Wet the back of the leather with a sponge or cloth. You do not want the front of the leather to be too wet. **(photo 1)** The core should be wet and soft, but the front just slightly damp – it should feel just cool to your hand and have a slight blush of dampness. If it gets too wet, allow to dry slightly.

To keep the leather from stretching, some experts like to mount their leather piece to illustration board using rubber cement. They place a thin coat of cement on the board, allow it to get almost dry and then place the dry piece of leather. The leather is then wet from the front, and allowed to dry to a blush appearance.

Apply the Pattern: Trace the pattern onto tracing paper. Position the traced pattern on the front side of the leather. Use a stylus to retrace the pattern, creating a marked pattern in leather. **(photo 2)**

Carve: The first thing to do is to carve the design using a swivel knife. (I find that everyone agrees on this.) Hold the knife at a slight angle with your thumb and the second finger on either side of the knife and your first finger on top to guide the swivel. Pull it along the marked pattern. **(photo 3)** When carving, a rule of thumb is to carve half-way through the leather.

Tool: Place the leather piece on a stone slab. Use the various stamping tools to shape and model the leather. The beveller is used first to bevel the carved cuts by placing the tool on the cuts and a smooth line is beveled along the cut. The mallet is used to strike the tool, creating an impression in the leather. **(photo 4)** This process gives definition to the design. Use other tools to add shading and texture to your work. **(photos 5, 6, 7, 8, and 9.)**

Finish: Stain or dye the leather if you wish. Coat the dyed or natural leather with a waterproof coating so that it will harden and retain the design.

These are photos of the Rose Trivet that appears in the Projects section of this book and shows examples of how various tools can be used.

Photo 1. Dampening the back of the leather with a sponge.

Photo 2. Tracing over a pattern with a stylus.

Photo 3. Cutting the rose outline with a swivel knife.

Photo 4. Use stamping tools to create the dimensional design. Beveling the edges of the rose and outlining with a beveler tool.

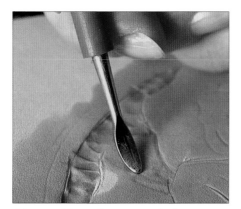

Photo 5. Using the spoon end of a modeling tool to shade the rose.

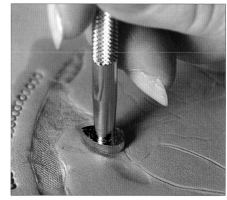

Photo 6. Adding more shading with a pear shader.

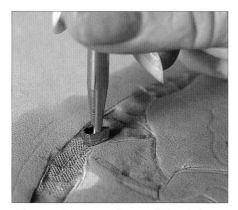

Photo 7. Stamping the area behind the rose with backgrounder tool.

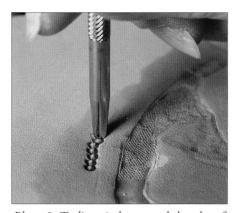

Photo 8. Tooling circles around the edge of the oval.

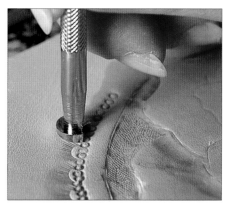

Photo 9. Tooling scallops outside the border.

Punching Holes

Holes need to be punched in leather for attaching metal hardware, for sewing, or for decoration. There are many types of hole punches available.

I found that the revolving punch with a variety of hole sizes is the most versatile – you simply slide the leather into the tool and squeeze. (**photo 1**) If you need to place a hole farther from the edge where the tool won't reach, simply place the hole cutting tube where you want it, then use a mallet to strike the tool.

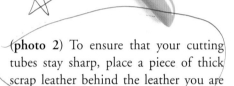

A revolving hole punch.

Photo 1. Using a revolving punch to make a hole.

Photo 2. Using a revolving punch with a mallet.

(**photo 2**) To ensure that your cutting tubes stay sharp, place a piece of thick scrap leather behind the leather you are punching.

Holes also can be made in leather with an awl, with individual hole and slot punches, or with hole chisels. Choose the tools you prefer.

Punching a Design

Follow these steps when punching a decorative, repeating design:

1. Punch the design on paper to make a pattern.

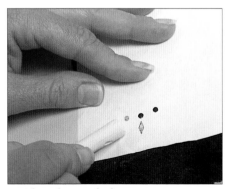

2. Place the punched paper pattern on top of the leather you want to punch. Rub chalk in the holes, marking the design on the leather.

3. Remove the paper pattern and punch where indicated by the chalk marks.

Setting Metal Hardware
Such as Snaps, Rivets & Grommets

Metal hardware is used to hold leather items or parts of items together and for decoration. To set hardware, you will need a setter, a hole punch, and a mallet.

This example shows a snap being set. There are four pieces to each snap pair – two pieces for the male part and two pieces for the female part.

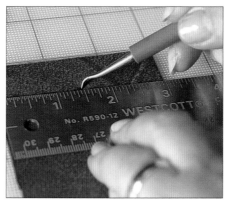

Photo 1. Mark the leather where the hardware is to be placed, using an awl, a stylus, or a piece of chalk.

Photo 2. Punch a hole with the hole punch of your choice. Here, I'm using a rotary punch.

Photo 3. Be sure to choose the proper size hole for your hardware. If you make too big a hole, the hardware will not stay in place as well.

Photo 4. Place the anvil (provided with setter) on your work surface, and place the front of one pair of snaps in the anvil. Slip the hole over the post of the snap.

Photo 5. Place the back part of that pair on the post, sandwiching leather between the two pieces of the snap.

Photo 6. Place the setter on the end of the post. Use the mallet to strike the setter. This locks the two pieces together.

Photo 7. Repeat with the corresponding two pieces to complete the snap.

LEATHER CRAFTING PROJECTS

This section of this book includes instructions for making 50 items
from leather. Projects range from home decor items such as pillows and
potholders, to a lampshade, and a footstool. There's also jewelry, tabletop
and desk accessories, and clothing items, plus journals, purses, and totes.
Some projects are very simple; others are more complicated – there's
something for every skill level, and a variety of styles and looks.
Each project includes photographs, a list of supplies and tools
needed, and step-by-step instructions. Where needed,
patterns are included as well.
They are the work of the talented designers who created them:
Patty Cox, Karen Embry, Lisa Galvin, Jacqueline Lee, Mary Lynn
Maloney, Barbara Mansfield, Barbara Matthiessen, Ann Mitchell,
and Karen Mitchell.

SUPPLIES

For the shade:

Lampshade frame (with vertical posts)

Kidskin (goat rawhide), enough to cover the frame

Leather hole punch

Leather lacing

Spring clothespins

2-prong lacing needle

Kraft paper

Scissors

For the stenciled design:

Vellum (for the stencil)

Craft knife

Spray mounting adhesive

Wedge-shaped makeup sponge

Rust colored chalk

Clear polyurethane spray finish

For the leather feathers:

Scrap leather

1-1/2 yds. leather lacing

Leather dyes - Turquoise, saddle tan, dark brown

Brushes (for applying dye)

Old toothbrush (for spattering)

3 beads

Craft knife

Scissors

Glue

Newspaper

Large jump ring

RAWHIDE LACED LAMPSHADE

By Patty Cox

This simple leather lampshade would look at home in variety of home decor styles. It's made of goatskin, which is dampened and stretched over a frame. I used clothespins to hold the damp skin to the frame while it was stitched and dried. Designs may be added to the inside or outside of the lampshade with acrylic paints, leather dyes, colored pencils, chalk, or charcoal. This frame includes a longhorn design that was stenciled with chalk. For permanence, it's a good idea to spray pencil, chalk, or charcoal designs with a polyurethane spray finish.

You can make the leather feathers to ornament the shade. Attach them to the lacing with a jump ring or, if your lamp fixture has a chain pull, you could attach them to the pull.

INSTRUCTIONS

Make Pattern & Cut Out Leather:

1. *If you are recovering an old lampshade,* remove the cover from the shade and use it to make a pattern. Add 1/8" along the top and bottom of the pattern for the hide to roll over the frame.

   If you are covering a new frame, roll kraft paper out on your work surface. Mark one vertical bar of the frame (so you will know when the frame has made a complete rotation). Slowly roll the shade frame on the kraft paper and mark with a pencil along the top and bottom bars of the frame. Add 1/8" along the top and bottom of the pattern for the hide to roll over the frame. Fit pattern to frame to make sure it fits.

   - The "backbone" area of a hide (where the animal's spine was) has the least stretch when wet and shrinks slightly more than the rest of the hide as it dries. If you use this area of the hide, add 1/8" allowance to top and bottom of that "stripe" before cutting the hide.
   - If the sides of your frame are straight, your pattern is ready.
   - If your frame curves (as my frame does), make compensations in your pattern to accommodate the curve.

2. Cut out kidskin with scissors.

Cover Frame:

1. Mark lacing holes 3/8" from top and bottom edges, spacing them 7/8" apart. Where the ends meet, mark holes 7/8" along one end, 1/4" from edge. Offset holes along other end, 7/8" apart and 1/4" from edge.

2. Punch holes, using a leather punch.

3. Soak kidskin in the bathtub for about 30 minutes. Remove softened skin from water and blot with a towel to remove excess moisture.

4. With the smooth side out (the smooth side is the outside of the skin), gently

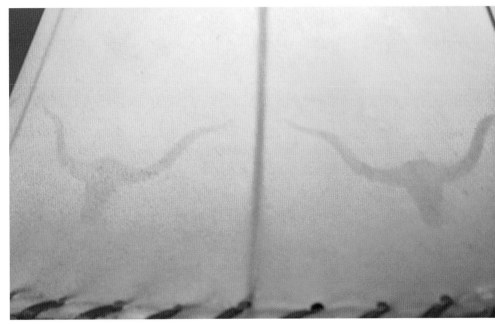

The stenciled design.

roll the skin over the frame, pull tautly over the top and bottom, and secure with clothespins. Be sure the skin overlaps the top and the bottom of the frame – the skin will shrink about 5% as it dries and the frame may be exposed if skin doesn't sufficiently cover the frame when it's wet.

5. Cut a length of lacing about three times the circumference of the shade bottom + three times the circumference of the shade top. Load the 2-prong lacing needle with lace.

6. Knot one end of the lace. Beginning from the inside top, carefully pull lacing through hole, wrap over shade top, and thread lace through next hole. Continue stitching shade top. *Tip:* After completing a whipstitch, hold the stitch with a clothespin while you move to the next stitch.

7. Stitch shade sides.

8. Stitch shade bottom, working in the same direction as you did on the top. Knot lace end. Allow shade to dry overnight.

9. Remove clothespins.

Stencil:

1. Trace longhorn pattern on vellum. Cut out stencil with a craft knife.

2. Spray a light coat of spray mounting adhesive on back of the vellum stencil. Position on the inside of lampshade.

Continued on next page

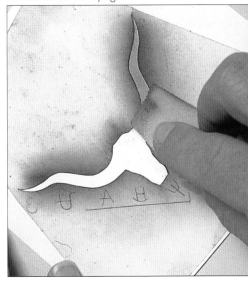

Stenciling the longhorn design with a wedge-shaped makeup sponge.

continued from page 23

3. Rub a makeup sponge in rust chalk. Rub sponge over stencil. Reposition stencil and continue.

4. Spray finished shade interior with a light coat of clear finish. Allow to dry overnight before using.

Make the Rawhide Feathers:

1. Using scrap hide, cut out three feather shapes with scissors.

2. Using a craft knife, score the center quill of each feather on the rough side of the hide. Score diagonal feather barb lines on each side of the quill.

3. Soak hide feathers in water 15 minutes.

4. Remove and lay on newspaper. Paint dye on both sides of damp feathers – turquoise on the top and saddle tan on the bottom. Spatter with dark brown leather stain. Let dry.

5. Cut out small v-shapes from each side of feather.

6. Cut three 18" lengths of leather lacing. Thread a large holed bead on each lace. Glue end of lace on each feather quill top. Slide bead over lace and quill.

7. Braid three laces together. Knot end.

8. Attach knotted end of braid to inside of lampshade lacing with a large jump ring. ❏

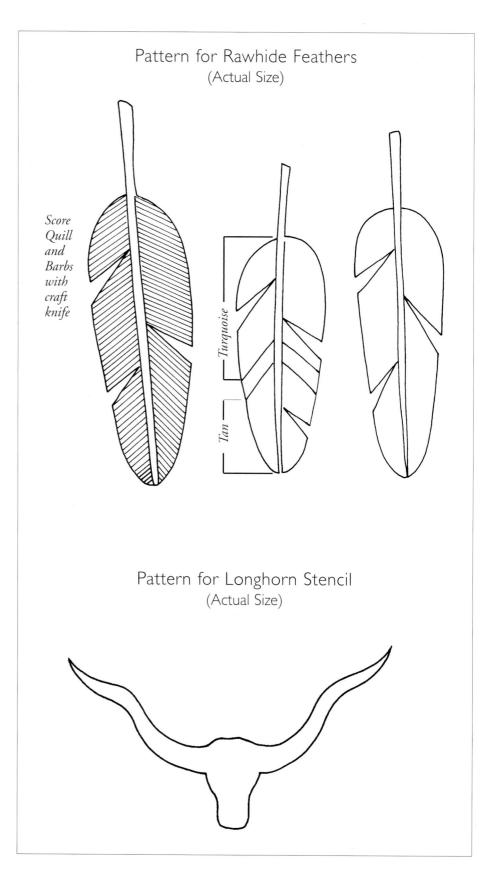

Pattern for Rawhide Feathers
(Actual Size)

Score Quill and Barbs with craft knife

Turquoise

Tan

Pattern for Longhorn Stencil
(Actual Size)

SUPPLIES

Leather:

Dark brown velvet suede,
26" square

Gold velvet suede, 18" square

Other Supplies:

Pillow form, 16" square

TOOLS

Cutting mat

Straight edge

Rotary cutter with straight and
decorative blades

1/16" hole punch (hand or drive)

Measuring tape

Clothespins

Yarn needle

Scissors

White chalk

SOFT SLEEP PILLOW

By Barbara Matthiessen

The leather lacing strips (you cut them yourself using a rotary cutter) are both decorative and functional. The ends are tied at the corners and they hold the cover together.

INSTRUCTIONS

Cut:

1. Place cutting mat on work surface. Use the straight blade in rotary cutter with a straight edge to cut an 18" square.
2. Using the same blade, cut four 3/4" x 26" strips from brown suede.
3. Use a decorative edge blade in the rotary cutter to cut a 16" square from gold suede.

Assemble:

1. Center gold suede on brown suede. Clip clothespins around edges to hold in place.
2. Make a chalk mark every 1" on gold suede. Use either a hand punch or drive punch to make a hole at every chalk mark.
3. Cut one end of each brown strip at a

sharp angle to ease insertion into needle. Start in one corner with the leather strip on top, leaving a 5" to 6" tail. Stitch in and out of punched holes with a simple running stitch until you reach the next corner. Pull leather strip out of the needle, allowing excess to hang for now. Repeat to stitch two

adjacent sides.
4. Tie overhand knots with leather strips in the two completed corners.
5. Slide in pillow form.
6. Stitch remaining side.
7. Tie corners. Trim corner strips to desired length. ❏

LEATHER & HOBNAIL FRAME

By Barbara Matthiessen

Supple red suede covers a wide wooden photo frame. The corners are decorated with rows of brass upholstery tacks.

SUPPLIES

Leather:
Red suede, 12" x 24"

Other Supplies:
Wooden frame, 8" square
16 hobnail upholstery tacks
Leather cement

TOOLS

Cutting mat
Craft knife
Straight edge
Chalk
Hammer
Old credit card or piece of mat board cut to same size for spreading cement
Needlenose pliers

INSTRUCTIONS

Cover Frame:

1. Place cutting mat on work surface. Cut two pieces from suede, one piece the same size as the frame's outside dimensions for the back cover, the other piece large enough to cover the front of the frame and wrap around the sides to the back.

2. Remove photo backing from frame. Place frame in center of front cover. Use chalk to draw around inside opening and mark from corner to corner with an X. (**photo 1**) Place the frame on the back cover and, using chalk, mark the frame opening.

3. On the front cover, cut an X in chalked opening and cut to within 1/8" of the traced lines in the corners. (**photo 2**) On the back cover, cut out along chalked line. Reserve the cutout piece.

4. Cover front of frame with cement. Place front cover on frame, aligning openings, and smooth into place.

5. Trim corners. (See photo 2.)

6. Apply cement to sides and edges of back of frame. Wrap leather around one side of frame, folding at corners. (**photo 3**).

Continued on page 28

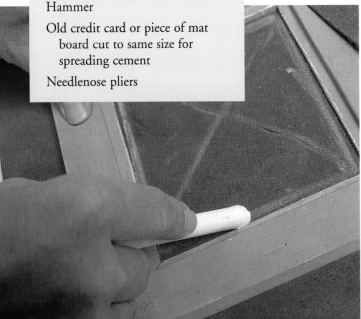

Photo 1. Marking the suede for the front cover.

Photo 2. Cutting the suede inside the frame opening.

Continued from page 26.

7. Working one flap at a time, spread glue on the flap and pull it through the opening to the back. (**photo 4**) Trim off the tips as necessary.

8. Work around the frame, securing the center flap and the side with cement. (**photo 5**)

9. Apply cement to back of frame. Align back cover and smooth into place.

10. Apply cement to reserved suede cutout. Apply to photo backing.

Trim:

Hammer tacks at frame corners. For each tack, hold the stem of the tack with pliers and hammer until the tack holds. Remove pliers and continue hammering until tack is flush with surface. Repeat with remaining tacks. ❏

Photo 3. Gluing one corner on the back side.

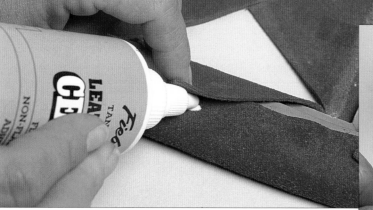

Photo 4. Gluing one flap from the center.

Photo 5. Gluing another side in place.

SUPPLIES

Leather:

Scraps of four colors of leather

Other Supplies:

Canvas photo frame

Black acrylic craft paint

Leather cement

TOOLS

Cutting mat

Straight edge

Rotary cutter with straight blade

Measuring tape

Paint brush

Old credit card or piece of mat
board cut to that size for
spreading cement

MOSAIC FRAME

By Barbara Matthiessen

Four strips of leather overlap at the corners of a frame to make a leather mosaic. Mix and match colors and textures as you like – this frame is a great way to use scraps from other projects.

INSTRUCTIONS

1. Paint frame black on all sides. Allow
   paint to dry.
2. Place cutting mat on work surface. Use
   a straight edge, rotary cutter, and
   measuring tape to cut all leather. Cut
   strips of all leathers to fit frame as
   shown in photo, making strips slightly
   narrower than frame and as long as
   each side.
3. Spread cement over back of one leather
   strip. Place on frame.
4. Spread cement on second piece. Place
   on frame, overlapping one corner on
   end of first piece.
5. Repeat with remaining two strips. Let
   dry. ❏

FOOTSTOOL WITH STYLE

By Lisa Galvin

You can build this footstool from the instructions provided or use this technique to re-cover a stool or chair seat in your home. Because of the durability of upholstery leather and the classic color combination, this is an accent piece you can enjoy for years.

The stool shown is 11-1/2" wide × 17-1/2" long and 12" tall.

Instructions follow on page 32.

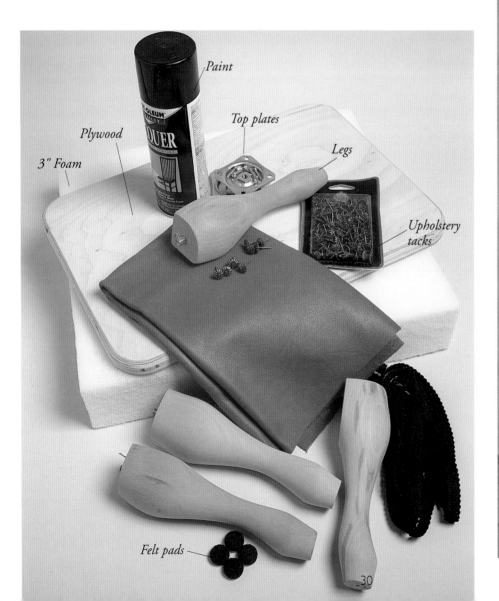

Paint

Top plates

Plywood

Legs

3" Foam

Upholstery tacks

Felt pads

30

SUPPLIES

Leather:

5 sq. ft. red upholstery leather

Other Supplies:

For the stool, if you're building it:

3/4" birch veneer plywood, 2 ft. x 2 ft. board (available at home improvement stores)

Black high lustre lacquer spray coating

4 Queen Anne style wooden legs, 8" tall

4 heavy-duty straight top plates with screws (available at hardware stores)

4 heavy-duty self-stick felt furniture pads, 3/4"

150-175 antique daisy upholstery tacks, 3/4"

For the cover:

Leather finish

Foam, 3" thick, 15" x 17" (or to fit)

3 layers polyester batting, 27" x 25" (or to fit)

3 yds. decorative braid, 1/2" wide

Contact cement

Self-adhesive vinyl shelf paper

TOOLS

Pencil

Band saw

Router equipped with 3/8" round-over bit

Sandpaper, extra fine grit

Steel wool, 0000

Tack cloth • Masking tape

Permanent marker

Straight edge or yardstick

Utility knife

Staple gun and 3/8" staples

Drill with drill bit for screws

Screwdriver

Polymer-head mallet or tack hammer

Leather shears • Scissors

INSTRUCTIONS

Construct Stool:

1. Enlarge pattern for stool top so top measures 11-3/4" x 17". Transfer pattern to plywood piece and cut out, using a band saw.
2. Use a router equipped with 3/8" round-over bit to round off the top edges of the board.
3. Lightly sand any rough edges from plywood and wooden legs. Wipe with a tack cloth to remove dust.
4. Tape the metal straight plates flat on a covered work surface, leaving at least 8" between them. Cover plates with self-adhesive vinyl shelf paper. Use a pencil to punch through vinyl at screw holes.
5. Screw legs on plates so the legs will stand vertically without falling over.
6. Spray paint legs and bottom side of board with black lacquer, following manufacturer's instructions. Let dry. Lightly rub with steel wool and wipe with a tack cloth. Repeat, applying a total of three to four coats of lacquer. Let dry completely.
7. Unscrew legs and remove shelf paper to reveal unpainted plates. Replace legs on plates, screwing them firmly in place.
8. Position plates with attached legs on the bottom (painted) side of wood, approximately 1" from edge. Align for placement and direction legs will be facing. Mark screw holes with pencil and drill pilot holes for screws. Remove plate from one leg and screw to plywood base. Screw leg back on and align. Repeat for all. Remove legs and set aside. *Tip:* Due to variations in screw threads and plates, it's a good idea to use a permanent marker to number the top of each leg and each plate. Numbering the legs and plates saves time and aggravation when reattaching them.

Pad the Top:

1. Use a straight edge and utility knife to cut the foam to fit the stool top.
2. Brush cement on the wood (**photo 1**) and position foam on the stool top. Trim corners with scissors to round slightly.
3. Stack batting layers and place on a flat surface. Turn stool top with attached foam upside down and center on batting. Pull batting tightly over foam and wooden top. Staple 1/2" from edge on bottom side, stabilizing points on each side. (**photo 2**) Continue stapling batting to base, pulling tightly and working side to side, end to end. Finish by stapling corners. Trim excess batting. *Tip:* An extra set of hands is helpful when covering and stapling – one person can pull tightly while the other operates the staple gun.

Cover:

1. Cover prepared base with leather, stretching the leather to fit snugly, easing corners as you work. Because of the close proximity of plates to corners, a few extra staples in some areas may be necessary. Trim excess leather.
2. Sit on a carpeted floor and hold the stool top on its side between your legs to stabilize it. Use a mallet or tack hammer to affix a row of decorative tacks all the way around base of stool.

Finishing:

1. Turn stool on its top. Trim away excess batting and leather around edges.
2. Cement two rows of decorative braid to cover staples and raw leather edges. Fold raw end of braid under 3/8" and cement in place.
3. Screw on legs. Attach felt pads to bottoms of legs. Turn stool upright.
4. Spray leather with leather finish to protect. ❏

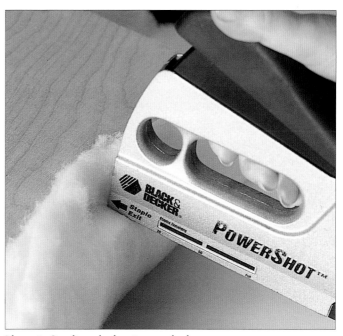

Photo 1. Brushing cement on the top to hold the foam in place.

Photo 2. Stapling the batting on the bottom.

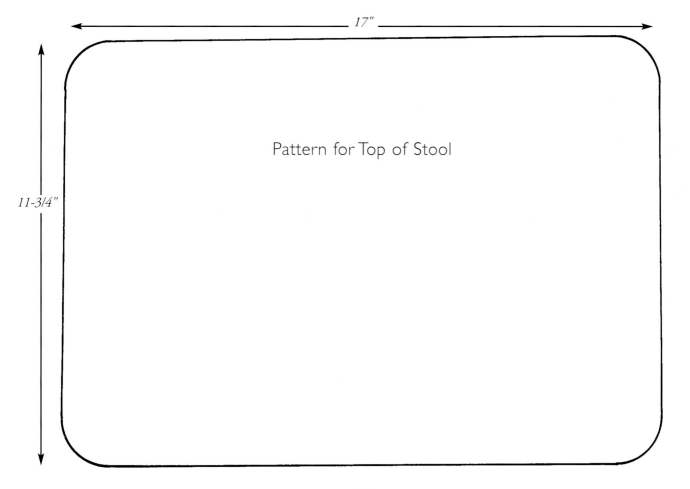

17"

11-3/4"

Pattern for Top of Stool

BRANDED LOG CARRIER

By Lisa Galvin

This sturdy leather log carrier is branded with designs that were created with a woodburning tool. (A woodburning tool is often referred to as a "branding tool" when it is used on leather.) It would make a wonderful "hearthwarming" gift.

Instructions follow on page 36.

SUPPLIES

Leather:

9 sq. ft. of 4-5 oz. vegetable tanned leather

Other Supplies:

Antique leather stain - Mahogany

Black waxed thread

Leather finish

Acrylic craft paints - Black, metallic olive, metallic sunset gold

Clear acrylic sealer, matte finish

2 lengths of oak dowel rod, 3/4" diameter, each 15-5/8" long

Contact cement

TOOLS

Rotary cutter

Cutting mat

Straight edge

Ruler

Drive punch (size 1), 3/32"

Punchboard

Mallet

Craft knife

Scissors

Woodburning tool with rounded flow point tip and teardrop-shaped shading tip

Pliers

Metal baking tray

Fine-grit sandpaper

Rubber gloves

Sheep's wool scraps

Plastic or paper to cover work surface

Paint brushes - #2 flat, #1 script liner

Sewing needle with large eye

2 yardsticks or 1/2" dowels 36" long

INSTRUCTIONS

Paint the Dowels:

1. Paint 3/4" oak dowels with two coats of black acrylic paint. Let dry.
2. Spray center of each dowel (approx. 8" section) with 2 coats of matte sealer. Set aside to dry.

Cut & Punch Leather:

1. Using a rotary cutter, mat, and straight edge, measure and cut a rectangle measuring 34" long x 16" wide.
2. Enlarge the pattern-punch template for tote ends so it matches the 16" tote width. Glue template to poster board.
3. Align pattern-punch template to one end of leather rectangle, matching corners. Use binder clips to hold in place. Place on punchboard and use 3/8" drive punch and mallet to punch two double rows of stitching holes.
4. Cut out handle hole, using a craft knife.

Woodburn Designs:

Practice the woodburned designs on a scrap piece of vegetable tanned leather or poster board before burning your project.

1. Screw shading tip into wood burning tool. Plug tool in outlet to heat up.
2. Lay tote piece with right side up onto a flat surface. Measure 17" from one end of tote to find bottom center. Place straight edge 1" from one side edge. Beginning at bottom center and using straight edge as a guide, brand the leaf-like border with the tips of the leaves facing upward toward handle. Return to bottom center and brand to opposite handle. As necessary, remove the charred buildup that accumulates on branding tips by rubbing tips lightly with sandpaper. Repeat on other side edge.
3. Randomly brand insects and pine cones with pine boughs on the tote, using the photo as a guide for placement. Brand the pine cones and insect bodies with wings using the shading tip. Change to the rounded tip for the pine boughs, pine cone stems, and insect heads. Return to the shading tip to create pine needles, antennae, and insect flight lines.
   - Additional depth and dimension can be created by rocking the shading tip on the leather – try a "heel to toe" or side-to-side motion.
   - The more pressure you apply to an area, the darker (and deeper) the image or edge will become.
   - The tip of the wedge shape is used to brand tiny dots around pine cone, at side border, and on insects' antennae.
   - Use pliers to remove hot tips and set tips on a metal tray to cool.

Stain:

1. Cover work surface with paper or plastic. Put on rubber gloves.
2. Pour some stain on sheep's wool. Rub stain on leather, spreading the stain quickly and evenly over the surface, working in a circular motion. Add more stain to wool as needed to cover entire surface and edges. Let dry completely.

Paint:

1. Use a flat paint brush to add light hints of olive green paint over pine needles, leaf-like border, and insect bodies.
2. Use the flat brush to add hints of sunset gold to pine cones and insect wings.
3. Use a script liner to add a few sunset gold highlight lines to pine cones and insect bodies and antennae. Let dry.
4. Spray tote with one to two coats of leather sheen to protect. Let dry.

Stitch:

1. Cut 100" of waxed thread and thread through needle. Working one end at a time, fold handle ends to match the stitching holes on other side of the handle opening. Use binder clips to hold in place.
2. Stitch through stitching holes, using double-back stitch. Start between the layers, bringing the needle up through

the back side of one hole near the handle opening. Leave a 4" length of thread to tie off later. Going through both layers, stitch over and under, working your way along the punched rows, returning to the starting point. Double back (hence the name), so the stitching lines appear as a constant line, and return to starting point. Tie thread ends in a knot and trim excess.

3. Cement seam.

4. Repeat on other side.

Glue Dowel Handles:

1. Slip dowel into pocket and cement to hold firmly in place. Slip two 1/2" dowels or yard sticks through handle opening. Place heavy books, a log or some weight inside tote and suspend between two tables or chairs. Allow to hang for two to three hours. (This will hold the handle dowels firmly to the tops of the handle pockets while the cement sets.) Remove weights and 1/2" dowels or yard sticks. ❑

Pattern for Tote Ends & Punching Template

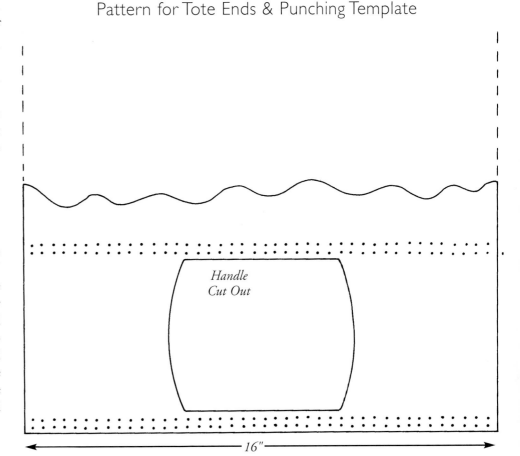

Handle Cut Out

16"

Sample of Branded Designs

TOOLED ROSE TRIVET

By Patty Cox

This project is a good way to become acquainted with the craft of leather tooling.
See the section on "Tooling Leather" in the Leather Crafting Skills section of this book for
photos and information on tooling techniques.

SUPPLIES

Leather:

7-1/4" square of 3-4 oz. tooling leather

Other Supplies:

4 silver corner plates

Mailing tape

Optional: Mat board, rubber cement

TOOLS

Stylus or awl

Modeling tool with spoon modeler at one end and a stylus at the other

Basic 7 Tooling Set *or* these tools - Swivel knife, beveler, seeder stamp tool, backgrounder, camouflager

Sponge and water

Mallet

INSTRUCTIONS

Prepare:

1. Press mailing tape on back of leather to keep it from stretching while you tool the design *Option:* Rubber cement the leather to a piece of mat board.
2. Dampen leather with water.
3. Position and tape pattern on leather top. Trace over pattern with stylus.

Tool the Design:

1. Cut rose outline and oval border with swivel knife.
2. Bevel edges with beveler tool.
3. Use spoon end of modeling tool to model the rose.
4. Use the pear shader to draw and model the rose shading.
5. Stamp the area behind the rose with the backgrounder.
6. Tool small circles with the seeder tool around the oval edge.
7. Tool scallops around outside edge, using the camouflage tool.
8. Position metal corner plates and strike with mallet to secure. ❏

Pattern for Tooled
Rose Trivet
(Actual Size)

TRIANGULAR PILLOW

By Lisa Galvin

This elegant tasseled pillow is an unusual, eye-catching accent piece. It can be sewn on a sewing machine, just like a fabric pillow. Rubber stamping is used to decorate the buttons.

Instructions follow on next page.

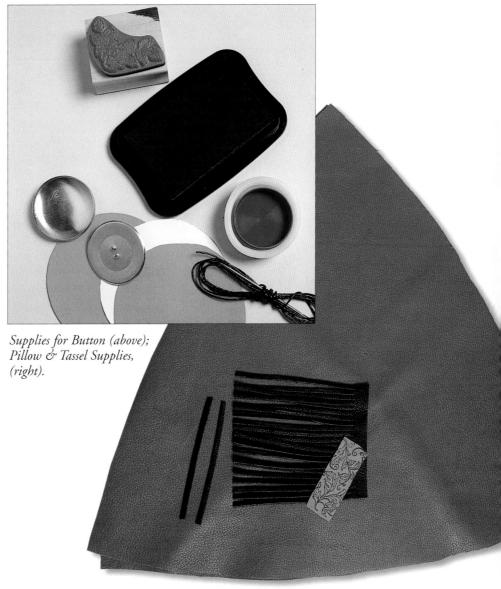

Supplies for Button (above); Pillow & Tassel Supplies, (right).

SUPPLIES

Leather:

4-1/2 sq. ft. red upholstery leather

Gold velvet pig suede,
 9-3/4" x 3-3/8"

18" length of 4" Deer tan Fringe in
 Black

24" black round lacing, 1mm

Other Supplies:

24" black waxed thread

Leather finish

Rubber stamp with leaf design

Polyester pillow stuffing

Acid-free archival solvent inkpad -
 Black

2 buttons to cover, 1-1/2" (3.8 cm)
 with button maker and pusher
 Red upholstery or nylon thread

Contact cement

TOOLS

Rotary cutter

Cutting mat

Craft knife

Leather shears

Sewing machine with size #18
 leather needle

Binder clips

Scratch awl

Mallet

Punchboard

3" darning needle

INSTRUCTIONS

Make Pillow:

1. Enlarge pattern and glue to poster
 board.
2. Using binder clips, clip pattern to red
 leather. Cut two pieces for pillow.
3. With front sides together, machine

Pictured left to right: Cut length of fringe for tassel with one strand folded to form a loop; rolled tassel; finished tassel.

stitch around pillow beginning and ending at dots on pattern. Leave area between dots open for turning and stuffing. **Do not** back stitch – knot thread ends to secure and add a drop of glue to hold.

4. Turn pillow right side out and stuff. Set aside. **Do not** close opening at this time.

Make Buttons:

1. Press inkpad on bottom of stamp. Stamp on gold velvet pig suede, applying even pressure. Lift stamp straight up to remove. Reapply ink and repeat until surface of suede is stamped.
2. Cover buttons, following manufacturer's instructions.
3. Roll side edges of covered buttons over the inkpad to create a dark ring that highlights the stamping.

Sew Buttons:

1. Cut waxed thread in half, creating two 12" strands. Thread two raw ends through eye of needle.
2. Slip needle through loop at back of button and pull through, leaving 6" of thread on each side of loop. Tie a knot.
3. Insert needle all the way through center of pillow and pull through on opposite side. Remove thread from

needle, and return to first side.

4. Thread remaining thread ends through needle and pull through pillow to opposite side.
5. Slip second covered button on two strands of thread. With the other two strands of thread tie a square knot, pulling tightly to anchor button at center. Tie a second knot to secure. Trim thread ends so they are concealed under button.

Cement Opening:

Cement seam allowance at side opening of pillow closed. Use binder clips to hold until set.

Make Tassels:

1. Cut three 5" lengths of deer tan fringe.
2. Fold one strand up and over top edge to create a loop. Cement on back to hold in place.
3. Apply cement to connecting band at fringe top and begin rolling top edges into a tight coil.
4. Cut a 1" x 3" piece of stamped gold suede. Apply cement to back of suede and around top of tassel. Wrap suede piece around tassel, folding top edge over to meet loop.

5. From remaining fringe, cut one strand of fringe. Apply cement to back side and wrap around suede.

6. Roll top edge of tassel on inkpad to darken and accent.

7. Repeat steps 2 through 6 to make two more tassels.

Attach Tassels:

1. Using scratch awl, mallet, and punch-board, punch a small hole at each out-side corner of the pillow.

2. Cut an 8" length of round lacing. Fold in half to make a loop on one end. Pull looped end 1" through punched hole at one corner. Bring ends of lace through the 1" loop and pull tightly, cinching to corner.

3. Thread one end of lace through tassel loop. Tie a square knot with opposite end securing tassel about 1/4" from pillow corner. Wrap ends of lace around 1/4" section of connecting lace. Tie a square knot, add a drop of glue to secure ends, and trim excess.

4. Repeat steps 2 and 3 to attach remaining tassels.

Finish:

Spray both sides of pillow with leather finish. ❏

Pattern for Pillow
Enlarge @ 250% for actual size.

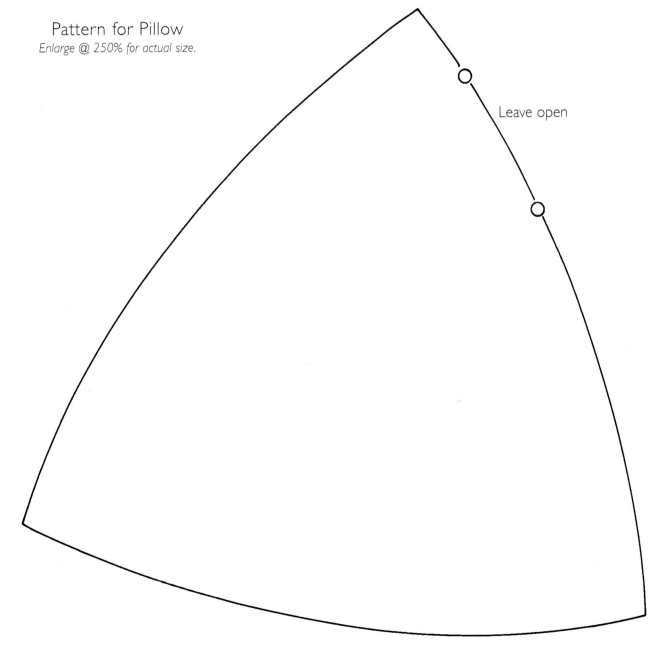

Leave open

TRIO OF POT HOLDERS

By Patty Cox

Leather is an unexpected but durable material for pot holders. These are decorated with rubber stamps and simple motifs cut from compressed sponges. They also look great on the table under hot serving dishes. And they can even be washed when made from suede.

Stamped Swirls Pot Holder

SUPPLIES

Leather:
Sueded cowhide, 7" x 7"
Black pigskin, 8" x 8"
5" leather lacing

Other Supplies:
1/2" wide masking tape
Rubber stamp - Swirl motif
Stamp pad - Black
Craft foam (to create your own stamp design)
1/4" dowel *or* craft knife
2 pieces silver ironing board cover cloth, 6-7/8" x 6-7/8"
1 piece fleece batting, 6-7/8" x 6-7/8"
Thread

TOOLS

Rotary cutter or leather shears
Pinking shears
Sewing machine with leather needle

INSTRUCTIONS

Decorate:
1. Run masking tape along two edges of the 7" square of suede as a guide for keeping swirl design straight. Rubber stamp swirl design.
2. Cut a triangle from craft foam using the triangle pattern given. Mount foam on a piece of dowel for a handle, or simply hold the foam stamp with the tip of a craft knife blade. Move the masking tape guide in 3/8". Stamp triangles along the edge of the hide. Let dry.

Assemble:
1. Place one piece of silver cloth on the black pigskin, shiny side down.
2. Place the batting on top of the silver cloth, then top with another piece of silver cloth, shiny side up. Tape in place with masking tape.
3. Machine stitch 1/4" from the edge through all layers, securing the padding to the pot holder.
4. Place decorated cowhide square on top of silver cloth.
5. Fold the 5" leather lace in half, forming the hanging loop. Place hanging loop in top corner, under hide. Sew hide to pigskin inside the border.
6. Trim edge of black pigskin 1/8" from cowhide square, using pinking shears.
❑

Pictured on opposite page, top to bottom: Stenciled Chicken Pot Holder, Painted Cross Pot Holder, Stamped Swirls Pot Holder. See additional instructions on page 46.

Patterns for Swirls & Triangle Border
(Actual Size)

Painted Cross Pot Holder

Pictured on page 45

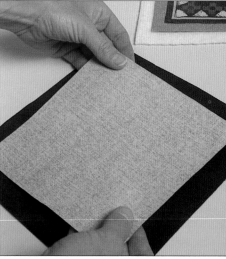
Photo 1. Placing the silver cloth square on the black pigskin square.

SUPPLIES

Leather:

Sueded cowhide, 7" x 7"

Black pigskin, 8" x 8"

Sueded cowhide, 5" x 3/8"

Other Supplies:

2 pieces silver ironing board cover cloth, 6-7/8" x 6-7/8"

1 piece fleece batting, 6-7/8" x 6-7/8"

Acrylic craft paints - Black, turquoise, country red

1/4" masking tape

Thread

Compressed sponge

TOOLS

Hole punch

Rotary cutter or leather shears

Pinking shears

Craft knife

Sewing machine with leather needle

INSTRUCTIONS

Decorate:

1. To make the border mask, run two rows of masking tape 1/8" apart along the edges of the 7" cowhide square.
2. Cut a cross and a triangle from a compressed sponge, using the patterns provided. Use hole punch to punch a hole in the center of the cross.
3. Sponge border inside masking tape with black paint.
4. Use the sponge cutout to stamp the cross design with turquoise paint.
5. Use the sponge cutout to stamp the triangles with country red. Let dry.

Assemble:

1. Place one piece of silver cloth on the black pigskin, shiny side down. See photo 1.
2. Place the batting on top of the silver cloth, then top with another piece of silver cloth, shiny side up. Tape in place with masking tape.
3. Machine stitch 1/4" from the edge through all layers, securing the padding to the pot holder.
4. Place decorated cowhide square on top of silver cloth. Photo 2 shows all the layers.
5. Sew hide to pigskin on each side of the black border.
6. Trim pigskin 1/8" from edge of cowhide square, using pinking shears. ❑

Photo 2. The layers of the pot holder before assembly. Shown top to bottom: Decorated cowhide, silver cloth, batting, silver cloth, and black pigskin.

Stenciled Chicken Pot Holder

The Stenciled Chicken Pot Holder is a variation of the Painted Cross Pot Holder. To make it, mask off and stamp a border with the sponge shapes and use a purchased stencil (I used a chicken, but any simple motif will do) to stencil a motif. I matched the red stencil paint for the chicken to the red leather backing piece.

Patterns for Cross & Triangle Border
(Actual Size)

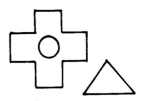

FLOWERED & FRINGED OVEN MITT

By Patty Cox

Leather dye is applied with a paint brush to create the fanciful floral design. The sturdy leather, silver cloth lining material, and fleece batting protect your hand when you work on a hot grill. Use a rotary cutter and a straight edge to make the decorative fringe.

Instructions follow on page 48

SUPPLIES

Leather:

2 pieces sueded cowhide, 11" x 14"

Other Supplies:

Rust thread

2 pieces silver ironing board cover cloth, 8" x 13"

2 pieces fleece batting, 8" x 13"

Leather dye - Oxblood red

TOOLS

Sewing machine

#16 sharp sewing machine needle

Small artist's paint brush

Rotary cutter and straight edge

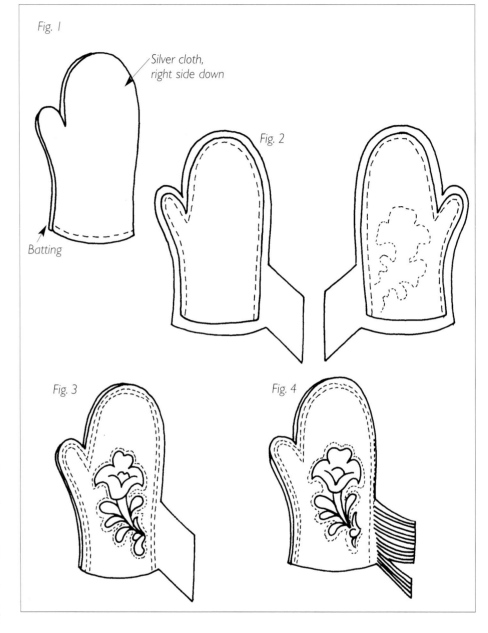

Fig. 1

Silver cloth, right side down

Fig. 2

Batting

Fig. 3

Fig. 4

INSTRUCTIONS

Cut Out & Decorate:

1. Transfer pattern for mitt outline to sueded cowhide. Cut out mitt front and back.

2. Photocopy flower pattern. Position and tape pattern on hide.

3. Set sewing machine to small stitch, then stitch scraps of leather to check stitch length and machine tension. Following the pattern lines, carefully through stitch paper and cowhide. Backstitch at the beginning and end of each line of stitching. Tear paper pattern away from hide.

4. Using a small artist's paint brush, paint leather dye inside stitch lines of design.

Make Padding:

1. Trim 1/8" from pattern on all edges and cut off fringe extension.

2. Stack pieces of silver ironing board cover cloth with right sides together. Using pattern, cut two lining pieces

from silver cloth.

3. Using same pattern, cut two pieces from fleece batting.

4. Place right side of silver cloth facing batting. Machine stitch 1/4" from wrist edge only. (Fig. 1) Turn right side out. Repeat for other side of padding.

5. Position padding on inside of each mitt piece, with silver cloth facing out. Tape in place with masking tape.

6. Machine stitch 1/4" around each mitt

piece, securing padding to mitt. (Fig. 2)

7. Machine quilt 1/8" around painted design on mitt front.

Assemble & Cut Fringe:

1. Place mitt front over mitt back. Machine stitch around mitt 1/8" from outer edge, leaving wrist opening unstitched. (Fig. 3)

2. Cut fringe on extension with rotary cutter and straight edge. (Fig. 4) ❑

Pattern for Oven Mitt
Enlarge @150% for actual size.

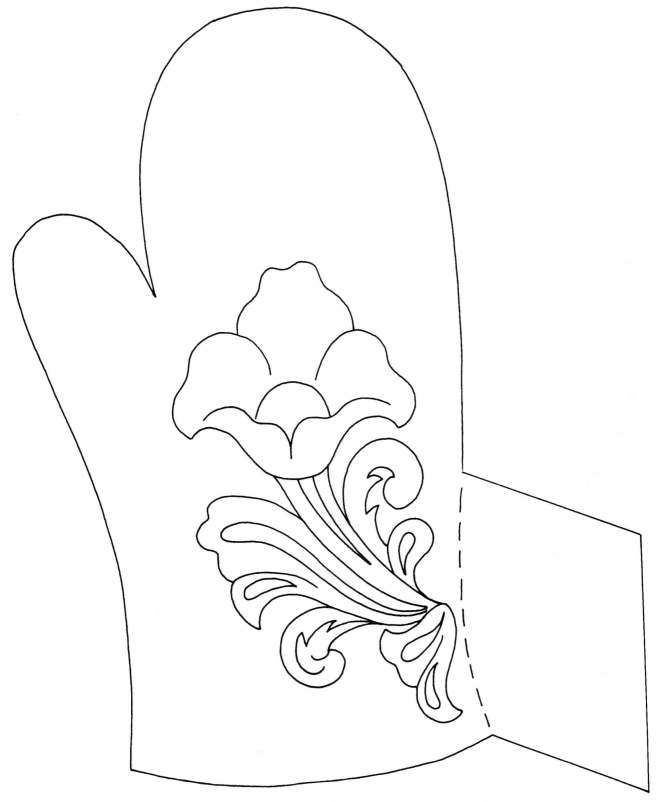

COWGIRL SPIRIT POT HOLDER

By Patty Cox

Show your cowgirl spirit with this colorful, fun pot holder. The design is painted with leather dyes. It is washable – wash and dry flat.

SUPPLIES

Leather:

Sueded cowhide, 7" x 9-1/2"

Red pigskin, 8" x 10-1/2"

5" leather lacing

Other Supplies:

Leather dyes - Oxblood red, turquoise, saddle tan

Thread

Fine tip permanent marker

TOOLS

Artist's paint brush

Rotary cutter or leather shears

Pinking shears

Sewing machine and leather sewing needle

Instructions follow on page 53.

Pictured top to bottom: *Cowgirl Spirit Pot Holder, Western Stitch Pot Holder*

Pattern for Cowgirl Spirit Pot Holder

(Actual Size)

continued from page 50

INSTRUCTIONS

Decorate:

1. Transfer pattern to cowhide rectangle.
2. Paint design with leather dyes, using the photo as a guide for color placement.

3. Outline letters and hat with black fine tip marker. Draw stitch lines in tan block.

Assemble:

1. Position painted rectangle on red pigskin.
2. Fold 5" leather lace in half, forming the hanging loop. Place hanging loop in top left corner, under cowhide rectangle.
3. Sew cowhide to pigskin – straight stitch 1/8" from the outer edge of the cowhide and inside the turquoise triangles border.
4. Trim pigskin 1/8" from cowhide edge, using pinking shears. ❑

WESTERN STITCH POT HOLDER

By Patty Cox

This pot holder design was inspired by stitch patterns on cowboy boots.
It's a simple, single layer of leather.

Pictured on page 51

SUPPLIES

Leather:

Sueded cowhide, 7" square

5" leather lacing

Other Supplies:

Rust thread

Leather dye - Saddle brown

TOOLS

Artist's paint brush

Sewing machine with leather needle

Pinking shears

Masking tape

INSTRUCTIONS

1. Photo copy pattern. Position and tape pattern on 7" cowhide square.
2. Set sewing machine to small stitch setting. Carefully stitch paper and cowhide following pattern line. Tie off thread ends. Tear paper pattern away from hide.
3. Fold a 3/8" x 5" strip of cowhide in half for hanging loop. Place loop under top corner.
4. Stitch a 1/4" border around the edge of the pot holder. Stitch over loop while stitching border.
5. Paint leather dye inside stitch lines of design and along outer border. Let dry. ❑

Pattern for Western
Stitch Pot Holder
(Actual Size)

HEART'S DESIRE STITCHED PILLOW

By Patty Cox

Two layers of leather are used to make this simple pillow. The heart cutout is handstitched with black lacing. The natural edge of the kidskin hide, positioned on the pillow front, adds textural interest.

SUPPLIES

Leather:

Gold kidskin, about a 13" square with uneven edge

Tan leather, 13" x 26"

Black waxed lacing

Other Supplies:

Pillow stuffing

Tan thread

Glue stick

TOOLS

Tapestry needle

Awl

Mallet

Sewing needle

Sewing machine with leather needle

Leather shears

INSTRUCTIONS

Cut:

1. Cut two 13" squares from tan leather.
2. Position gold kidskin diagonally over one square of tan leather, using the photo as a guide. Trim sides of kidskin evenly with tan leather square.
3. Trace heart pattern and enlarge on graph paper or a photocopier.
4. Transfer heart pattern to gold kidskin. Cut out heart.
5. Using the glue stick, tack the gold kidskin in place on the tan leather square. Lay leather flat on cutting surface.

Sew:

1. Mark stitch hole placement around heart.
2. Punch holes with awl.
3. Thread tapestry needle with lacing. Whipstitch around heart as shown in photo.

4. Place pillow front and back with right sides together. Machine stitch 1/4" from edges, leaving a 2" opening along the bottom edge.
5. Turn pillow right side out. Stuff with batting.
6. Hand stitch opening shut with tan thread. ❑

Pattern for Heart
Enlarge @200% for actual size.

ASIAN INFLUENCED COVERED BOX

By Jacqueline Lee

Supple lightweight red suede makes a striking cover for an oval papier mache box. It takes on an Asian look with the addition of frog closures (purchased at a fabric store) and black cording trim.

SUPPLIES

Leather:

Lightest weight red suede, enough to cover size of box you have chosen

Other Supplies:

Oval papier mache box with lid

2 black frog closures, 1 small and 1 medium

Flat black cording, 5mm wide, measure box to determine amount needed

Acrylic craft paint - Black

Matte acrylic sealer

Leather cement

TOOLS

Paint brushes

Cutting mat

Rotary cutter

Straight edge

Pencil

Tape measure

INSTRUCTIONS

Paint & Seal:

1. Mark a line on the box base at the bottom of where the lid overlaps.
2. Paint above that line on the outside of the box base, the inside of the box base, the inside of the lid, and the bottom of the box base with black acrylic paint. Let dry.
3. Seal all the painted areas with matte acrylic sealer.

Cut & Glue:

1. Using the lid as a template, trace its outline on the leather. Cut out the leather oval and glue it to the lid.
2. Cut a strip of leather as wide as the height of the lid rim and as long as the lid circumference. Glue the strip to the outside rim of the lid.
3. Cut a strip of leather as wide as the height of the box base below the marked line and as long as the circum-

ference of the base. Glue this strip around the lower part of the box bottom.

Decorate:

1. Cut and glue pieces of black cord around the top edge of the lid, around the bottom edge of the lid, and around the bottom of the box base.

2. Glue the medium frog on top of the box.

3. Glue the small frog on the side of the box, with half on the lid and half on the base as shown in the photo. ❏

PAISLEY PILLOW

By Mary Lynn Maloney

Velvety pigskin suede is used to decorate a jewel-tone cotton canvas pillow cover. Metallic paints, brilliant colors, glass beads, and beaded fringe are combined for 60s-retro look.

SUPPLIES

Leather:
1/2 yd. purple velvet pigskin suede
1/2 yd. rust velvet pigskin suede
2 yds. lilac suede lacing

Other Supplies:
Canvas pillow cover, 18" x 18"
Fabric dyes - Golden yellow, turquoise, azure blue
Metallic acrylic paints - Halo blue, gold, pearl violet, pearl blue
Pillow form, 14" x 14"
Assorted glass matte beads with large holes
Iridescent purple/amber beaded fringe, 13"
Transfer paper

Leather cement
Fabric glue

TOOLS

Shallow plastic container
Rubber gloves
Large & small paint brushes
Hand-held rotary cutter
Metal-edge ruler
Paper towels
Circle template
Fine point permanent marker
Scissors
Clothes dryer

INSTRUCTIONS

Paint Pillow Cover:
1. Put on rubber gloves. Lay canvas pillow cover in shallow plastic dish and paint randomly with yellow dye.
2. Turn over pillow cover and apply random spots of turquoise dye. Follow with random spots of blue dye. Turn over pillow and repeat.
3. Hang pillow to dry, protecting floor with newspapers. When dry, heat set for 15-20 minutes in clothes dryer.

Add Leather:
1. Cut the purple pigskin suede into an 8-1/2" x 12-3/4" rectangle, using the ruler and rotary cutter. Use cement glue to adhere purple suede, suede side up, to pillow cover.
2. Transfer the paisley images to the rust pigskin suede.
3. Paint three paisley images with the metallic paints, using the photo as a guide. Let dry.
4. Cut out paisley shapes with scissors. Use leather cement to glue them on the purple suede.
5. Use the circle template and fine-line marker to draw four circles of various sizes on rust suede. Transfer random sections of the paisley images in the circles.
6. Cut out circles with scissors. Adhere to right side of the pillow cover with leather cement.
7. Draw and cut out 14 circles of various sizes from the purple suede.
8. Adhere the purple circles, smooth side up, on top of the rust circles and randomly over the rest of the pillow, using leather cement. Let dry.

Assemble:
1. Using fabric glue, adhere beaded fringe to purple suede piece. Let dry.
2. Insert pillow form in pillow cover.
3. Cut four 12" pieces of lilac suede lace.
4. Tie one piece around one corner section of the pillow flange. Secure in place by putting a dab of leather cement between the suede lace and the pillow cover fabric.
5. Cut 2" up the length of the ends of the lace, creating a split in each dangling end. String one or two beads on each split end and gently knot each end. Add a touch of leather cement at each knot.
6. Repeat steps 4 and 5 at the remaining corners. ❏

Pattern for Paisley Pillow
Enlarge @125% for actual size.

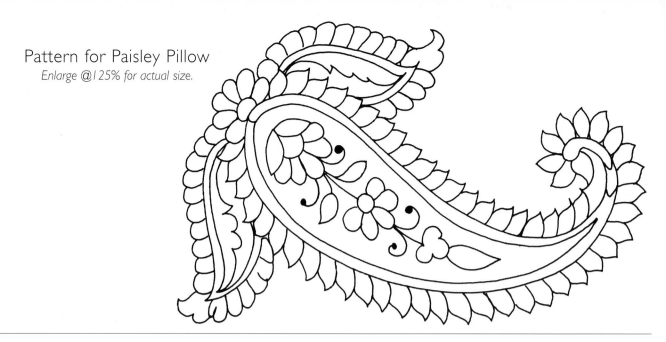

STAMPED PHOTO FRAME

By Lisa Galvin

Salvaged scrap suede trim pieces come to life when used to decorate an inexpensive frame, converting it to a stylish piece of art. Layers of suede and rolled suede "beads" add dimension to the flat surface. The idea can be adapted to fit any frame and your favorite rubber stamps.

SUPPLIES

Leather:

1 sq. ft. gold velvet pig suede   1 sq, ft. purple velvet pig suede
Red pig suede trim piece, 3" x 6"

Other Supplies:

Burgundy or red-tone wooden picture frame (This one measures 8- 1/4" x 10-3/8" and has a 5" x 7" opening.)

Acid-free, archival solvent ink

3 rubber stamps, your choice

Rub-on finish - Ebony

Heavy poster board to fit frame opening

Leather cement

TOOLS

Sandpaper	Tack cloth	Soft cloth
Plastic glove	Make-up sponge	Leather shears

INSTRUCTIONS

Prepare Frame:

1. Sand frame lightly to dull the finish. Wipe away dust with tack cloth.
2. With a gloved hand, use a makeup sponge to apply ebony rub-on finish, concentrating the color on the outer edges and corners. Let dry briefly, then buff with a soft cloth. Let dry completely.

Cut & Stamp Suede Pieces:

1. Measure and cut four gold suede pieces to fit the front of the frame. Let 1/4" of the frame show around each piece.
2. Rubber stamp the top and bottom pieces with one stamp and the sides with another stamp.
3. Adhere suede to frame.
4. Cut two strips purple velvet suede 1/2" narrower and 1" shorter than the top and bottom gold suede pieces.
5. Rubber stamp the purple strips with the same motif used on the top and bottom gold suede pieces. Cut into trapezoid shapes and glue to gold suede.
6. Stamp various small pieces of gold and red suede and adhere to top and bottom parts of frame, using the photo as a guide.
7. Cut five 1/4" x 3-1/2" strips of stamped suede in varying colors. Beginning on one end, roll each length to make a tiny-coiled "bead". Glue end to hold. Glue three on frame as shown.

Make Inset:

1. Cut a piece of heavy poster board to fit inside frame.
2. Cut a piece of purple suede to fit poster board and glue to poster board. Place inside frame.
3. Glue remaining leather "beads" to covered inset. ❏

CELTIC-INSPIRED BOX

By Jacqueline Lee

A Celtic-motif rubber stamp supplied the design inspiration for this elegant suede-covered box. The stamped design is mounted on a sturdy leather square that provides a visual frame.

SUPPLIES

Leather:

Lightest weight gold suede, enough to cover size of box you have chosen

Heavyweight black suede, scrap piece

Other Supplies:

Rectangular wooden box with hinged lid

Rubber stamp - Celtic knot motif

Permanent black ink pad

Acrylic craft paint - Black

Matte acrylic sealer

Leather cement

TOOLS

Paint brushes

Cutting mat

Rotary cutter

Straight edge

INSTRUCTIONS

Paint:

1. Use black acrylic paint to paint the inside, bottom, and all edges of the box. Let dry. Apply a second coat.

2. Apply matte sealer to all the painted areas. Let dry.

Add Suede:

1. Cut two strips of gold suede to cover the sides of the lid and the base. Center and glue the strips around the top and bottom sections of the box. Black painted edges should be visible on either side of each strip.

2. Cut a rectangle of gold suede to fit the top of the lid. Center and glue the suede rectangle on the lid.

Add the Stamped Motif:

1. Stamp the Celtic motif on a small piece of gold suede, using permanent black ink. Let dry.

2. Cut out the motif, leaving a 5/8" border around the edges of the image.

3. Cut a slightly larger square of black suede.

4. Center the stamped square on the black square and glue together.

5. Center the layered Celtic motif on the front of the box. Glue in place, being careful to apply glue only to the top portion of the motif's back side. ❑

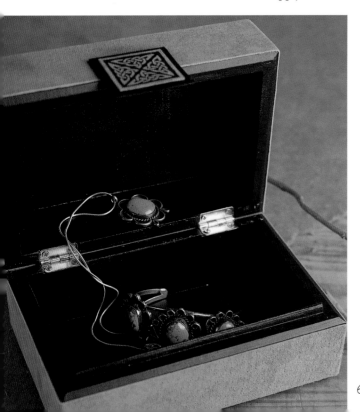

STAMPED PENDANT NECKLACE

By Karen Mitchell of AnKara Designs

Metallic paint is rubber stamped on dyed leather cutouts and laced together with leather braid to make an unusual necklace. The pictured necklace is 16" long but could be elongated with additional leather pieces.

SUPPLIES

Leather:

1 piece vegetable-tanned 3-4 oz. leather, 4" x 6"

3 strips 3/32" wide kangaroo lace, 30" each, dark brown

Other Supplies:

Glue stick

4 index cards, 4" x 6"

Rubber stamp - Sunburst motif, 1-1/4" square

Acrylic craft paint - Metallic bronze

Waxed thread - Dark brown

Clear cellophane tape

Leather dye - Oxblood

Contact cement

Leather sheen

Bead with 1/4" hole

TOOLS

Scissors

White pencil

Pencil sharpener

Cosmetic sponge

Fine-tip paint brush

Paper towels

Big eye needle

Leather dye applicator

Leather shears

Mallet

Poly punching board

Awl

INSTRUCTIONS

Dye:

1. Lay the 4" x 6" piece of vegetable tanned leather on a protective piece of plastic or paper on your work surface. Apply a coat of oxblood dye to the entire surface. Allow to dry.
2. Apply a second coat. Allow to dry completely.

Cut Pieces:

1. Photocopy the two pattern pieces. Use the glue stick to adhere each piece to an index card. Cut out the pattern pieces.
2. Trace around the pendant pattern piece once and trace around the side piece six times, using the sharpened white pencil.
3. Mark punch holes with awl as indicated on the pattern pieces.
4. Cut out the pendant and the side pieces, using leather shears.

Stamp:

1. Place the seven pieces on a sheet of paper to protect your work surface. Dip the cosmetic sponge in bronze paint and apply an even coat over the surface of the rubber stamp. Center the stamp over the front of the pendant and press firmly.
2. Apply paint to the stamp again. Center over the opposite end of the pendant and press firmly. Allow to dry.
3. Apply an even coat of paint to the stamp and lay the stamp with its pattern side up on the work surface. Center the first side piece over the pattern. Carefully press the leather on the stamp, then lift it away. Do not slide the leather, or you may smear the paint. Repeat for the other five side pieces. Allow to dry. Wash the stamp thoroughly.

4. With a fine-tip brush, paint the edges of the pendant and the six side pieces with bronze paint. Allow to dry.

Punch:

1. Place the punching pad on a hard surface. Place the pendant piece on the punching pad, right side up. Align the 5/64" hole punch with the awl marking at the bottom of the pendant back, at least 1/8" from the outside edge. Strike the punch with the mallet three or four times to make a hole. Repeat on all awl markings on the back and the front of the pendant. Make sure the holes are at least 1/8" from the edge.
2. Place the side piece right side up on the punching board. Align the 1/8" chisel with the first of the two awl markings on one end. Strike the chisel with the mallet three or four times to punch the slit. Align the chisel with the second awl marking, and strike with the mallet. If the slits do not meet in the middle, align the chisel to punch the center of the slit. Repeat for the other side of this piece. Punch the other five side pieces the same way.

Make the Braid:

1. Knot the three strands of kangaroo lace together at one end. Tape the knot to the edge of your work table. With the shiny side of the laces facing up, braid the three strands to form a tight, flat braid. When you reach the end, wrap it with a piece of tape.
2. Lay the braid on a piece of paper that protects your work surface. Dip the cosmetic sponge in bronze paint and

Continued on page 66

continued from page 64

lightly coat the front of the braid. When you have coated a 6" section, wipe off the excess paint with a paper towel, leaving a bronze patina on the leather. Continue painting and wiping the leather in 6" sections until the entire braid is painted. Allow the paint to dry completely.

3. Wrap a piece of tape around the center of the braided strand. Cut the braid in half in the middle of the tape. On one of the pieces, brush contact cement on the front side of the braid for a 1/4" strip next to the taped section. Turn the other piece so the braid lays in the opposite direction. If the inner end of the strand is the knotted end, wrap a piece of tape just below the knot and cut off the knot. Brush a 1/4" strip of contact cement on the back of the braid next to the tape. Allow the cement to set up.

4. Overlap the two sections of braid that were coated with cement and press them together, right sides of both facing up.

5. Cut an 8" piece of waxed thread. Wrap the glued section of braid six times, keeping the wrapping flat (do not overlap the thread as you wrap). Tie the ends of the waxed thread tightly, and trim the ends. Cut off the taped ends of the braid close to the wrapped section.

6. On the back of the wrapped section of braid, brush a coat of contact cement and allow it to set up. On the inside of the pendant, 1/16" below where the pendant folds in half, brush a 1/4" strip of contact cement and allow it to set. Apply the wrapped section of the braid to the inside of the pendant. Press firmly to adhere.

Stitch Around Pendant:

1. Cut off a 36" piece of waxed thread. Thread it through the big eye needle, double the strand, and knot the ends.

2. Starting on the upper right side of the folded pendant, pull the thread through the top punched hole on the front of the pendant, stopping when the knot reaches the hole. Pull the thread around to the back of the pendant. Stitch through both layers of the pendant, pulling the thread

back through the front. Whipstitch around the pendant, pulling the thread back to front through the second hole. Continue to whipstitch the right side of the pendant until you reach the second to last hole.

3. Take a running stitch from the second to last hole down to the bottom center hole, pulling the thread front to back. On the back side of the pendant, take a running stitch from the center hole to the second to last hole on the left side. Pull the thread from the hole on the left back to the center hole, pulling it front to back. On the back of the pendant, run the thread from the center hole to the second to last hole on the right, pulling the thread back through to the front. Stitch across from the hole on the right to the second to last hole on the left, and pull the thread through to the back. You should have a triangle of stitching at the bottom front of the pendant and a V-shaped stitching pattern on the back.

4. Continue to whipstitch up the left side of the pendant. When you get to the last hole on the upper left side, take an extra stitch and knot the thread. Trim excess thread with scissors.

Assemble:

1. Trim one taped end of the braided necklace strand at a 45 degree angle. Take the first dyed and stamped side piece and lace the braid through one slit on the side

piece. The braid should run from front to back, and then should be threaded from back to front at the opposite end of the piece. Repeat for two more side pieces, spacing the pieces on the braid as desired.

2. Add three side pieces to the braid on the opposite side.

3. For the toggle closure, determine on which side of the necklace you will put the bead, and which side the loop. To attach the bead, knot the braid 1/4" below where you would like the bead to sit. Slide the bead on the braid and knot the braid close to the bead on the opposite side. (The hole should not slide over the knot.) Trim excess braid.

4. Fold the braid on the loop side about 1/8" beyond where you want the final length to be. (The extra allows for the bulk of the braid that passes through the loop.) Determine the size of the loop needed to slide snugly over the bead. Mark the braid on the inside with the white pencil where the loop meets.

5. Paint a 1/4" strip of contact cement on the back of both parts of the braid below each white marking. Allow the cement to set. Press the two sections of braid together to form a loop, adhering at the cement.

6. Cut an 8" strand of waxed thread. Wrap the glued section of braid seven times and secure with a knot. Trim the excess thread and the excess braid from the folded over section. To wear the necklace, slide the bead through the loop. ❑

Patterns for Stamped Pendant Necklace
(Actual Size)

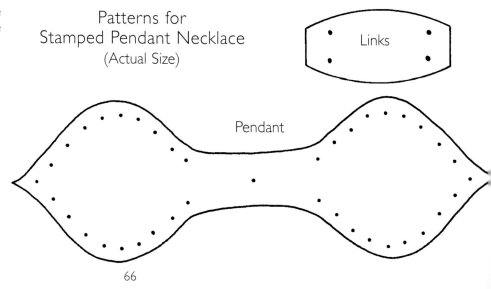

Links

Pendant

Patterns for Flower Barette
(Actual Size)

See page 68 & 69
for instructions and photo.

SUPPLIES

Leather:

2 pieces vegetable-tanned 3-4 oz. leather, 3" x 6"

1 piece vegetable-tanned 3-4 oz. leather, 3" x 3"

1 piece dark brown velvet suede, 3" x 3"

1 piece rust velvet suede, 3" x 3"

Other Supplies:

3-1/4" French barrette

5" strip beaded fringe

8 brass eyelets, 1/4"

Glue stick

Contact cement

Industrial craft glue

4 index cards, 4" x 6"

Leather dye - Oxblood

Leather sheen

TOOLS

Scissors

White pencil

Pencil sharpener

2 large paper clips

Leather dye applicator

Leather shears

Mallet

Poly punching board

Awl

Teardrop leather punch

Round leather punches, 5/32", 5/16"

1/4" eyelet setting tool

Small bowl

Rubber gloves

Wooden skewer

Patterns can be found on page 67.

INSTRUCTIONS

1. Photocopy all four pattern pieces. Use the glue stick to adhere each piece to an index card. Cut out the pattern pieces.
2. Dip one of the two 3" x 6" pieces of

FLOWER BARRETTE

By Karen Mitchell of AnKara Designs

Layers of punched leather are attached to a barrette to make an eye-catching hair ornament. A tassel made from beaded fringe spills out from the center.

vegetable tanned leather in a bowl of warm water to dampen it. Allow the leather to dry until it is only slightly damp. Carefully roll the leather, smooth side out, to give it some curve. Wrap a strip of index card over the edges of the leather and use a large paper clip to clamp the slightly curved leather on the barrette at each end. (The index card protects the leather from scratches.) Allow to dry completely. Remove it from the barrette.

3. Lay the second 3" x 6" piece of leather flat on a protective piece of plastic. Wearing rubber gloves, use the applicator to apply an even coat of oxblood dye. Let dry. Apply a second coat. Discard protective plastic. When the second coat of dye is almost dry, roll the strip, dyed side out,

to give it some curve. As you did with the first piece, clamp the dyed leather to each end of the barrette with paper clips, using strips of index card to protect the leather from scratching. Allow to dry completely.

Cut Pieces:

1. Lay the natural (not dyed) 3" x 6" piece flat on the table. Lay the base #1 pattern piece in the center of the strip and trace around the pattern with the sharpened white pencil. Cut out, using leather shears.
2. Center the base #2 pattern piece over the cutout base #1. Carefully and lightly trace the outline of base #2 on the smooth surface of base #1. Set aside.

3. Lay the dyed 3" x 6" piece of leather flat on the table. Place base #2 pattern on it and trace around it with the sharpened white pencil. Use the awl to mark leather at dots indicated on the pattern. Remove pattern. Cut out with leather shears.

Punch & Glue:

1. Place dyed base #2 piece of leather on the punching board. Align teardrop punch with dots at one end of the pattern, 1/8" from the point. Strike the punch firmly with the mallet three or four times to punch the leather.

2. Turn the teardrop punch to a 45 degree angle from the first punch hole, and align the tool with the dot markings. Strike with the mallet to make second hole. Align the teardrop punch with the markings for the third hole and punch.

3. Repeat the three punches on the opposite end.

4. Spread a thin coat of contact cement on the back of base #2. On the smooth front side of base #1, spread a thin coat of contact cement within the traced lines. Allow contact cement to set.

5. Center base #2 over base #1 and press the cement-coated sides together. Remove excess cement you see through the punch holes with the pointed tip of a wooden skewer by rolling it off of the surface of base #1.

6. Place the adhered bases, smooth sides up, on the punch pad. Using the 5/16" round leather punch, punch the center hole.

7. Re-align the punch with one of the four dots surrounding the center hole so the outside of the punch edge touches the dot. Use mallet to punch. Punch three more times, each time aligning the outside edge of the punch with one of the dots. (You will have a clover-shaped hole.)

8. Place the base on a piece of paper in a ventilated area and spray with leather sheen. Allow to dry completely. Set aside.

9. Spread a thin coat of contact cement on the back of the 3" x 3" piece of brown suede. Spread a thin coat of contact cement on the smooth side of the 3" x 3"

piece of vegetable-tanned leather. Allow to set.

10. Place the suede on top of the vegetable tanned leather, cemented sides together. Press out any air bubbles.

11. Center the rounded flower pattern on the brown suede. With the sharpened white pencil, trace around the pattern. Use the awl to mark the punch holes. Cut out the flower.

12. Place the flower on the punching pad, suede side up. Center the 5/32" round punch over one awl marking, making sure the punch is at least 1/8" from the outer edge of the petal. Punch a hole through the flower petal. Repeat to punch the other seven petals.

13. Install brass eyelets in the punched holes in the petals with the finished sides of the eyelets on the suede side.

14. Center the pointed flower on the back side of the 3" x 3" piece of rust suede. Trace around it. Use the awl to mark the center of the flower. Cut out the flower.

15. Spread a thin coat of contact cement on the circular center section on the front of the brown suede flower. Spread a thin coat of contact cement on the circular center section on the back of the rust suede flower. Allow cement to set.

16. Place the rust flower over the brown flower so the brown petals can be seen between the rust petals. Press the two flowers together, cement sides together.

17. Place the flower face up on the punch pad. Place the 1/8" chisel along the markings in the center of the flower. Punch a slit in the center of the flower. Move the chisel outward and punch a cross shape in the center of the flower. Set aside.

Add Beads:

1. Pull the beads off of the outer strand of the beaded fringe strip. Knot the thread to prevent the beads from coming off. Repeat on the other end.

2. Lay the fringe strip on a piece of paper. Spread a thin coat of contact cement on the tape edge of the fringe. Turn over the fringe and spread a coat of contact

cement on the other side. Allow cement to set.

3. Pull knotted thread ends up and out of the way. Carefully roll the fringe into a tassel. Fold under the end of the fringe to make a clean finish. Coat the edge of the fringe with another layer of contact cement and allow it to set.

4. Spread a coat of contact cement in a 1/2" circle at the center on the front of the flower. Allow cement to set.

5. Use the back end of a leather tool to open the cross-shaped hole on the flower, pushing the handle through the flower from the front. Push the tape edge of the tassel through the hole in the flower, pulling from the back. Pull the tassel until the beads are flush with the front of the flower. Press the leather around the tassel to adhere in place.

6. Spread a 1/4" circle of contact cement around the outside edge of the hole on the back of the flower and where the tassel protrudes through the hole. Spread contact cement on the inside edge of the hole punched in the base of the barrette, and in a 1/8" circle around the hole on the front side of the base. Allow cement to set.

Assemble:

1. Press the flower into the hole on the barrette base, aligning the leather tabs on the back of the flower with the clover shaped hole on the base. Make sure the flower is pressed in firmly to adhere.

2. Cut a 5/8" square of suede from the scraps. Spread a coat of contact cement on the back and let it set up. Spread a 5/8" square of cement on the back of the leather barrette base over the hole, and allow the cement to set. Apply suede square over the hole.

3. Squeeze a line of industrial craft glue on the surface of the barrette. Center the leather base over the barrette and press together.

4. Wrap a strip of index card around the leather at each end of the barrette and clamp the barrette to the leather with the paper clips until the adhesive is dry. ❏

SUPPLIES

Leather:

Heavyweight tan suede

Heavyweight black suede

Other Supplies:

Rubber stamp with horse motif

Permanent black stamp pad

4 pheasant feathers

Pin back

Ultra-fine point permanent black marker

Light tan marker

Artificial sinew - Natural color

2 metal feather charms

1 small shell with hole for stringing

Assorted small beads

TOOLS

Sturdy scissors

Leather hole punch

Leather cement

PREHISTORIC HORSE PIN

By Jacqueline Lee

A rubber stamp with a horse motif reminiscent of a cave painting makes an interesting, primitive pin when stamped on an irregular leather shape.

INSTRUCTIONS

Stamp & Cut:

1. Ink the horse stamp with permanent black ink and press on tan suede.
2. Mark an irregular shape around the horse and cut it out.
3. Color the body of the horse with a tan marker.
4. Enhance and lengthen the mane and tail with an ultra-fine point black marker.
5. Cut a slightly larger irregular shape from black suede.

Continued on page 72

STAMPED TRIBAL PIN

By Jacqueline Lee

A tribal figure stamped on a leather oval is layered on a larger leather oval, giving the appearance of a frame.

SUPPLIES

Leather:

Heavyweight tan suede

Heavyweight dark brown suede

Other Supplies:

Rubber stamp with tribal figure motif

Permanent black stamp pad

3 pheasant feathers

1 pin back

Leather cement

TOOLS

Sturdy scissors

Oval template

Leather hole punch

INSTRUCTIONS

Stamp & Cut:

1. Ink the tribal figure stamp and press it on the tan suede.
2. Using an oval template, center the stamped figure in an oval 1/4" larger than the image on all sides. Mark the outline.
3. Cut just inside the line using sturdy scissors.

Continued on page 72

continued from page 70

Add the Pin Back:

1. Center the pin back on the black piece and mark the leather at each end. Use the leather punch to make a hole at each mark.
2. Open the pin mechanism and thread the sharp pin and the clasp mechanism through the holes. (The working portion will stick through the holes on the back side of the broach. The base of the pin back will be hidden between the two layers.)

Decorate:

1. Cut two 4" lengths of sinew. Separate each strand into three or four segments.
2. Tie knots in the bottoms of five sinew strands and thread the beads, shell, and feather charms on each strand as shown. Tie knots above the beads. (You should have one long strand with beads and the shell, two strands of small beads, and two strands with feather charms and seed beads.)
3. Trim the strands, leaving a 3/4" tail of sinew above the upper knot and 1/16" below the bottom knot.
4. Glue the long tail of each bead strand to the back of the horse layer. Start by centering the longest strand beneath the horse.
5. Lay the piece face down. Glue the two beaded strands on either side of the long strand, leaving a 1/16" to 1/8" gap between the strands. Glue a feather charm strand next to each beaded strand, using the same spacing. Allow to dry.
6. Glue the pheasant feathers to front side of the black leather. Glue one feather to the left of the bead strands and two feathers, overlapping slightly, to the right side of the bead strands. Glue the final feather so it appears to arch over the horse. *Tip:* Hold the beaded front layer of the pin in place against the black back layer to determine where to place the feathers.
7. Glue the two layers together. ❑

STAMPED TRIBAL PIN

continued from page 71

4. Select a second oval that is one or two sizes larger than the one used for the figure. Mark the outline on dark brown suede. Cut out.

Add the Pin Back:

1. Center a pin back on the dark brown oval and mark the leather at each end. Use the leather punch to make a hole at each mark.
2. Open the pin mechanism and thread the sharp pin and the clasp mechanism through the holes. (The working portion will stick through the holes on the back side of the broach. The base of the pin back will be hidden between the two layers.)

Decorate:

1. Arrange the three feathers, overlapping slightly, at the top of the larger oval (on the side with the base of the pin back) and glue in place.
2. Center the tribal figure layer and glue in place. ❑

Pictured on this page: Notepad Cover and Business Card Holder.
Instructions follow on pages 74 - 79.

NOTEPAD COVER

By Mary Lynn Maloney

Layers of leather provide dimension and texture on a notepad cover. Rubber stamped motifs embellish the top layer.

SUPPLIES

Brown oil-tanned utility leather, 22" x 12"

Red velvet suede, 3" x 12"

Gold velvet suede, 4" x 12"

Brown suede lace, 14"

Other Supplies:

Leather cement

Fine point permanent marker

Rubber stamps - Spirals motif, triskel motif

Heat-set pigment inks - Brown, cranberry

Blank notepad, 5" x 8"

TOOLS

Hand-held rotary cutter

Metal-edge ruler

Scissors

Hair dryer

Patterns can be found on pages 78 - 79.

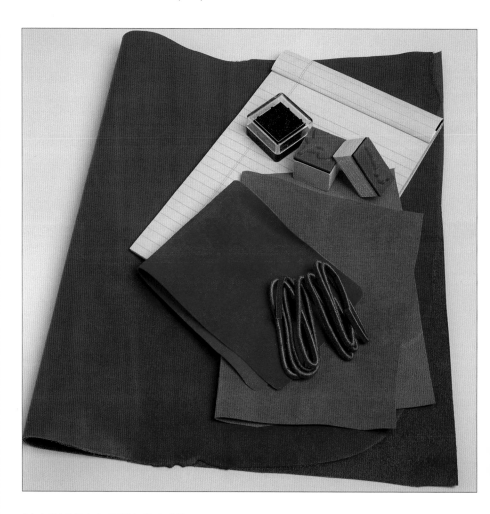

INSTRUCTIONS

Cut & Glue:

1. Enlarge pattern and cut out.
2. Using a fine point marker, trace pattern on brown leather. Cut out, using scissors for the curved edge and the rotary cutter and metal ruler for straight edges.
3. Fold the leather as indicated on the pattern to form the pocket that will hold the notepad. Use leather cement to glue the left-hand and bottom edges of the pocket. *Tip:* Use the notepad as a guide when creating the pocket opening.
4. Trace the gold decorative shape on gold velvet suede. Cut out with scissors.

5. Trace the red decorative shape on red velvet suede. Cut out with scissors.

Stamp:

1. With brown ink, randomly stamp the spiral image on the gold velvet suede.
2. With the cranberry ink, randomly stamp the triskel image on same piece. Heat set with a hair dryer for a few seconds.

Glue:

1. Apply a thin line of leather cement on the wrong curved side of gold velvet suede. Adhere to left edge of red velvet suede.

2. Beginning at one end of the brown suede lace, apply leather cement to approximately 3" of one side of the lace. Roll the lace into a tight spiral. Add more leather cement as needed to create the spiral size you desire. Hold with fingers until cement begins to set (about 20 seconds).
3. Repeat with the other end of the lace, forming a spiral in the opposite direction. Set aside to dry.
4. Use leather cement to glue the red and gold velvet suede piece to the left side of the cover, placing the piece over the spine and about 1" on the back of the cover. Leave the curvy edge unglued.
5. Apply leather cement to flat edges of the lace spiral. Attach to left side of the cover, using the photo as a guide. ❑

BUSINESS CARD HOLDER

By Mary Lynn Maloney

This leather business card holder stamped with a decorative motif is a perfect companion to the notepad cover. Whipstitching secures the pockets that hold the cards.

SUPPLIES

Leather:

Gold velvet suede, 5-3/4" x 4-1/4"

Red velvet suede, 3-1/2" x 10"

Brown suede lace, 4"

Scrap piece

Other Supplies:

Fine point permanent marker

Red poly/cotton all purpose thread

Small square of beeswax

Rubber stamp - Triskel motif

Heat-set pigment ink - Brown

TOOLS

Hand-held rotary cutter

Metal-edge ruler

Scissors

4-prong buckstitch chisel, 3/32"

Mallet

Pounding surface, such as a self-healing cutting mat

Glover's needle

Hair dryer

Leather cement

Patterns can be found on pages 78 - 79.

INSTRUCTIONS

Cut:

1. Trace the business card holder pocket pattern on red velvet suede.
2. Turn over pattern and trace again, creating a mirror image.
3. Cut out the pieces, using scissors for the curved edge and the rotary cutter and metal ruler for straight edges.

Punch & Stitch:

1. Cover the pounding surface with the piece of scrap leather. Lay the gold velvet suede on the surface, wrong side up. Line up the straight edges of one red velvet suede pocket, right side up, with the 4-1/4" side of the gold velvet suede. Beginning at the left side of the red velvet suede pocket, place the 4-prong chisel along this side, 1/8" from the edges of the leather pieces. Hold the chisel with one hand and hit the top with the mallet eight times, driving the chisel through both pieces of suede. Remove the chisel.

2. Place the first prong in the last hole created and punch again, going around three sides of the pocket.

3. Thread the glover's needle with a double 18" length of red thread. Knot the end. Run the thread between your finger and the square of beeswax to make stitching easier.

4. Whipstitch the edges through the punched holes, keeping the stitches firm but not too tight. Hide end knots between the two layers of suede.

5. Repeat on the other side.

Decorate:

1. Trace the decorative front curve pattern on the remaining red velvet suede. Cut out with scissors.

2. Using brown ink, randomly stamp the red suede with the triskel rubber stamp. Heat set with the hair dryer for a few seconds.

3. Fold and decide which side will be the front. Using leather cement, glue the stamped red suede piece to the front cover.

4. Beginning at one end of the brown suede lace, apply leather cement to approximately 1" of one side of the lace. Roll the lace in a tight spiral, adding more leather cement as needed to achieve the spiral size you desire. Hold with your fingers until the cement begins to set (about 20 seconds).

5. Repeat with other end of lace, forming a spiral in the opposite direction. Let dry.

6. Apply leather cement to flat edges of the suede lace spiral. Attach to front cover as shown in the photo. ❏

Pattern for Notepad Cover

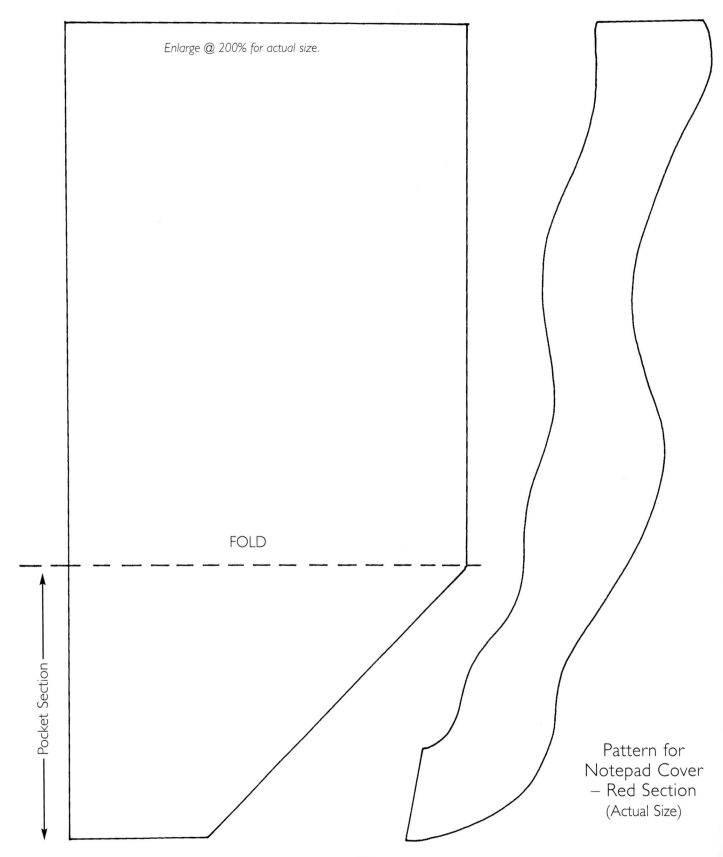

Enlarge @ 200% for actual size.

FOLD

Pocket Section

Pattern for
Notepad Cover
– Red Section
(Actual Size)

Pattern for Notepad Cover – Gold Section (Actual Size)

Pattern for Business Card Holder Pocket
(Actual Size)

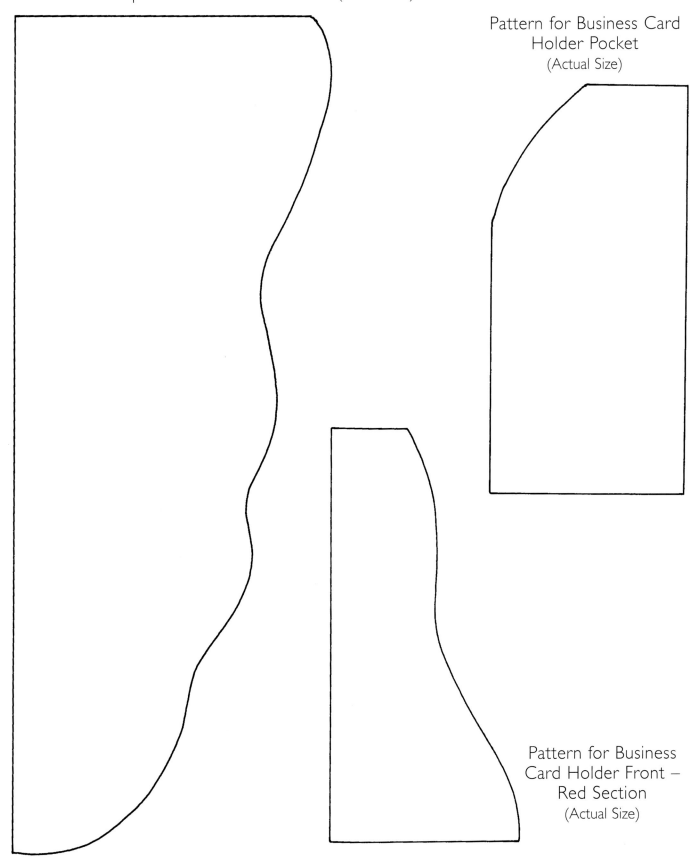

Pattern for Business
Card Holder Front –
Red Section
(Actual Size)

TOOLED BOOKMARK

By Ann Mitchell of AnKara Designs

Here's an easy project involving tooling, punching, and lacing.
For more information about tooling, see "Tooling Leather" in the
Leather Crafting Skills section.

SUPPLIES

Leather:

Vegetable-tanned 3-4 oz. leather, 2" x 7"

4 ft. kangaroo lace, 3/32"

Other Supplies:

Acrylic craft paint - Sage, dark brown, metallic bronze

Contact cement

Spray-on leather sheen

TOOLS

Paint brush

Leather shears

Mallet

Punching board

Granite, marble, tile, or other work surface

3-prong lacing chisel, 1/8"

2-prong lacing needle

Basic 7 tooling set (See the section on Tooling.)

Modeling tool (spoon on one side, stylus on the other)

Scissors

Small bowl

Sponge

Wooden skewer

Paper towel

INSTRUCTIONS

Cut & Prepare:

1. Photocopy pattern and cut out.
2. Cut a 1-5/8" x 6" piece of vegetable tanned leather, using leather shears.
3. Dip the leather piece in a bowl of warm water or wipe both sides with a moistened sponge – it should be uniformly damp on both sides. Allow the leather to dry slightly.

Punch:

1. Lay the pattern piece over the leather strip and, using the stylus end of the modeling tool, mark dots where the 3-prong chisel will be used. Mark the curves for the veiner tool.
2. Lay the leather piece on the punching board. Using the 3-prong chisel and the mallet, punch lacing holes.

Tool:

By now the leather piece should be dry enough to begin tooling – the inner core of the leather should be wet and the surface should feel fairly dry. If the leather dries out too much as you work, spritz it lightly with water or moisten carefully with a sponge, but don't get it overly wet – if you do, the impressions could fade.

1. Use the veiner tool to follow the marked curves and stamp, turning the tool to make the pattern.
2. Use the teardrop-shaped background tool to stamp three petal designs on the concave side of each curve.
3. Use the small round seeder tool to stamp a dot at the pointed tip of the center petal.
4. Use the spoon side of the modeling tool to tool a ridge behind each of the veiner tool designs. Allow to dry.

Add Paint:

1. Dip the tip of your finger in sage paint and gently rub the paint over the entire bookmark, being careful not to get paint in the tooled designs.
2. Rub metallic bronze paint over the sage paint. (The bronze is used as a highlight, so full coverage is not necessary.) Let dry.
3. Apply a thinned wash of brown paint to the tooled impressions with a brush. Wipe off the excess with a paper towel. Allow to dry.

Lace:

1. Cut three 14" pieces of kangaroo lace. Secure one end of one piece in the 2-prong lacing needle. Starting at the upper left hole on the back, use a running stitch through the punched lacing holes. Leave a 4" tail of lace on each end.
2. Fit the second piece of lace in the lacing needle. Starting on the front, lace down through the first center hole at the top of the bookmark and continue with a running stitch the length of the bookmark. Again, leave 4" tails on each end.
3. For the third piece, start at the back of the bookmark use a running stitch through the final set of holes, again leaving 4" tails.
4. Cut two 1" pieces of kangaroo lace for loops. Fold into thirds, overlapping the ends.
5. Using a wooden skewer, coat the back of one third of lace and the front of the overlapped third with contact cement. Allow cement to set. Press two ends together to form a complete loop. Repeat for the second loop.
6. Using the contact cement, glue each loop over the three tails of lace at each end of the bookmark. Place the loop about 1/2" from each end. Trim the lace ends so they are even. ❑

Pattern for Bookmark
(Actual Size)

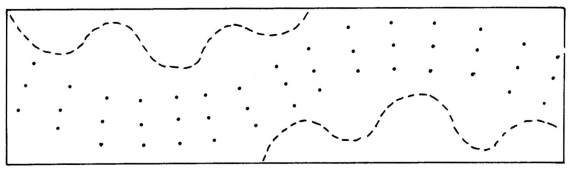

PUNCHED BOOKMARKS

By Lisa Galvin

Scrap pieces of suede left over from larger projects are terrific for creating bookmarks. Here, one punched design in many variations turns small pieces of suede into eye-catching bookmarks with contrast. Practice with construction paper to create unusual contrasting combinations with punched designs.

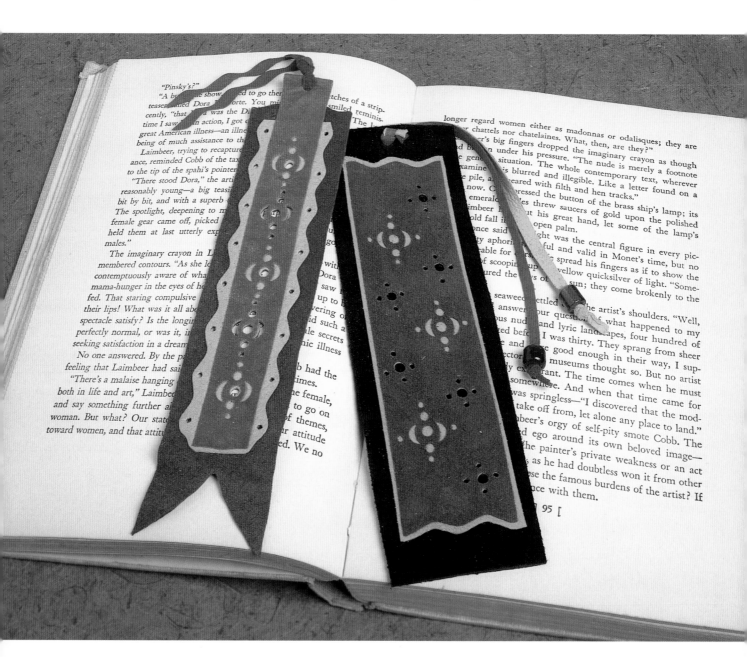

SUPPLIES

Leather:

Black cow suede piece, 2" x 6-3/4"

Velvet suede pieces - Red, purple, gold, 9-1/4" x 3-3/8"

Other Supplies:

2 purple glass beads with large holes

Contact cement

Poster board

Construction paper in various colors (for practicing)

TOOLS

Mini punch set with size 2 (1/8") and size 4 (5/32") tubes

Drive punch, size 9 (1/4")

Drive punch, half moon shape filigree

Poly cutting & punching board

Wooden mallet

Leather shears

Rotary cutter with straight and wave cutting blades

Cutting mat

Straight edge ruler

Craft knife

Large eye needle

Purple Background Bookmark

Black Background Bookmark

Instructions follow on page 84.

continued from page 83

INSTRUCTIONS

For bookmark with black background
Cut:
1. Using cutting mat and rotary cutter with straight blade, cut these pieces:
   Purple - 1-7/16" x 5-1/2", 1/8" x 9"
   Gold - 1-5/8" x 5-3/4", 1/8" x 9"
2. Cut top and bottom edge of purple piece with wave cutting blade.

Punch & Assemble:
1. Using the photo as a guide, punch **only** that portion of the design that shows gold behind the purple.
2. Glue purple piece to gold piece.
3. With shears, cut gold ends to match wave on purple, leaving a small border.
4. Punch remaining designs through both the purple and gold layers.
5. Glue to black background piece.
6. Use a needle to slip purple beads on 1/8" strips. Knot one end of each.
7. Punch a 1/4" hole at top of bookmark. Slip un-knotted ends through the hole and tie a knot to secure. Add a little glue on back to hold in place. ❏

For bookmark with purple background
Cut:
1. Using cutting mat and rotary cutter with straight blade, cut these pieces:
   Purple - 1-5/8" x 7"
   Red - 3/4" x 7-1/4"
2. Using wave blade, cut:
   Gold - 1-1/4" x 5-3/8"
   Purple - 1/8" x 7"
3. Use the wave blade to trim the top of the large purple piece.

Punch & Assemble:
1. Punch three design motifs on red suede piece in a column, leaving 1" between them.
2. Glue red suede piece to gold suede, leaving 1-1/2" of red extending above gold.
3. Glue gold piece to purple piece as shown in photo.
4. Going through all layers, finish punched design column by punching two additional design motifs between the ones you already punched.
5. Punch 1/8" holes at wave-cut extensions on gold.
6. Punch 5/32" holes at centers of the first three designs punched in the column.
7. Fold bookmark in half. Trim ends on the diagonal. Unfold.
8. Fold over red extension and glue to back of purple.
9. Punch a 5/32" hole through red loop at top. Fold purple wave-cut strip in half. Loop through hole. Pull to cinch, working knot down. Let glue dry. ❏

Patterns for Punced Bookmark – Design Motifs

KEY

● Size 2 (1/8") circle
● Size 4 (5/32") circle
○ Size 9 (1/4") circle

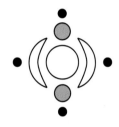

SUPPLIES

Leather:

Suede (enough to fit the footprints of the socks or slippers)

Thin leather lacing *or* embroidery floss

Other Supplies:

Knitted socks or slippers

Cardboard

Marker

TOOLS

Needle

Scissors

Pins

INSTRUCTIONS

Make Patterns & Cut:

1. Trace around foot on a piece of cardboard. Cut out foot shape.
2. To make the pattern for the leather soles, trace around the foot shape on another piece of cardboard. Use the

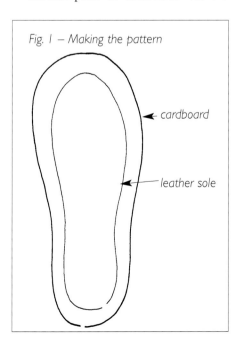

Fig. 1 – Making the pattern

← cardboard

← leather sole

SLIPPERS WITH A SOLE

By Patty Cox

It's easy to make a pair of cozy knitted slippers warmer and more durable with supple, sewn-on leather soles. And when they wear out, you can replace them!

If you knit or crochet, you can make the slippers, too, or simply add the leather soles to a pair of purchased thick wool socks.

marker to draw a smaller foot shape than the first pattern (about 1/2" to 3/4" smaller all around). Cut out to make sole pattern.

3. Place sole pattern on suede side of leather. Draw around pattern with marker. Reverse pattern, then draw another sole on suede side of leather. Cut out both soles.

Assemble:

1. Insert cardboard foot shape in one knitted slipper, lightly stretching slipper sole.
2. Place leather sole on slipper bottom, smooth side down. Pin in position.
3. Whipstitch using leather lacing or blanket stitch around leather sole with embroidery floss.
4. Repeat for other slipper. ❏

WINE BOTTLE GIFT BAG

By Patty Cox

A stained leather disc with a tooled grape leaf motif makes an understated decoration for a kidskin wine bag. Just add a bottle of your favorite wine and you'll have a perfect hostess gift.

SUPPLIES

Leather:

Kidskin leather, 12" x 14"

24" leather lacing

Tanned leather disc, 2" diameter

Other Supplies:

Leather stain - Walnut

Contact cement

TOOLS

Leather punch

2-prong lacing needle (optional, but helpful)

Basic 7 tooling set (See the section on Tooling.)

Sewing machine with leather needle

Sponge

INSTRUCTIONS

Make Bag:

1. Lay kidskin flat. Fold the uneven edge of hide over 2-3".
2. With the folded edge at the top, cut a 12" wide x 14" tall rectangle from kidskin. (Fig. 1) Open top fold.
3. Fold long right sides together. Machine stitch 1/4" seam along side and bottom. (Fig. 2)
4. Open inside bottom of bag as shown in Fig. 3. Sew a seam 1" in from each point.
5. Turn bag right side out. Fold top edge to outside, making bag about 10" tall.

Decorate:

1. Punch holes 1" from the top fold and 3/4" apart through both layers of folded hide. (Fig. 4) Thread lacing through holes.
2. Transfer pattern to leather disc. Use a sponge to wet both sides of the leather. Let dry until only slightly damp.
3. Tool design, following the instructions for "Tooling Leather" in the Leather Crafting Skills section. Let dry completely.
4. Stain with walnut leather stain.
5. Apply contact cement to back of tooled leather disc and on a 2" area on the front of the bag. Wait 10 minutes, then press tooled disc on bag front. ❏

Patern for Tooled Disk
(Actual Size)

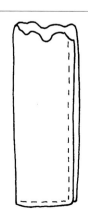

Fig. 1

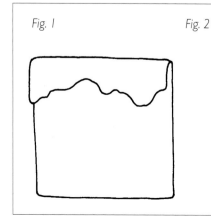

Fig. 2

Fig. 3

sew points & cut off

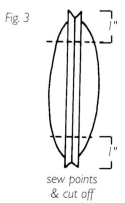

Fig. 4
Punch holes

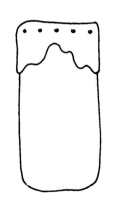

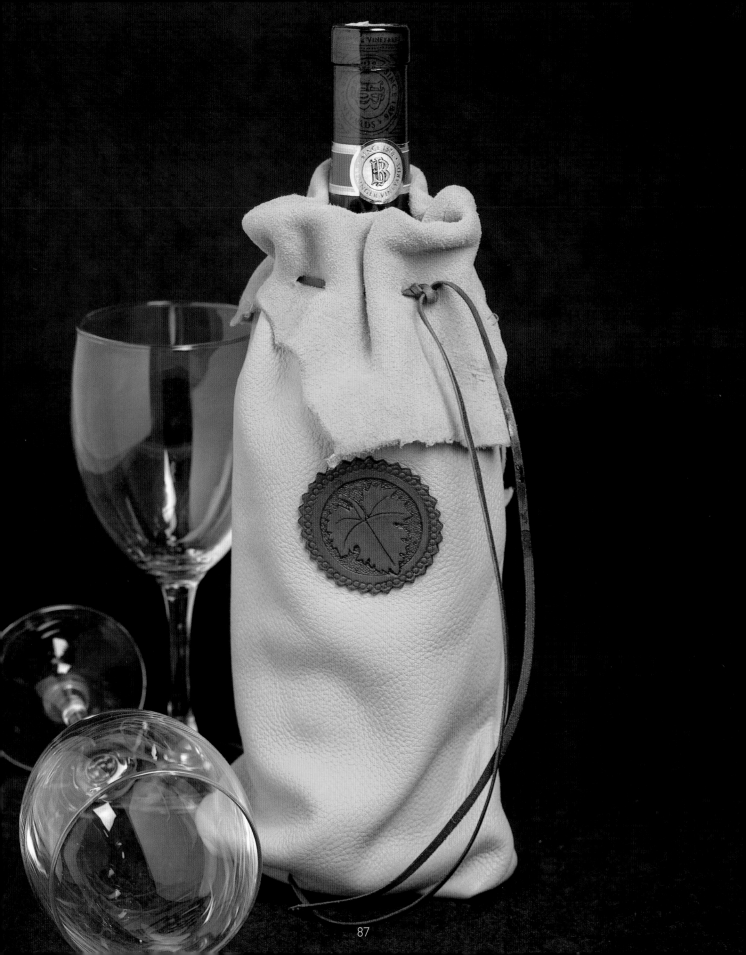

DESK ACCESSORIES

By Barbara Matthiessen

An ordinary blotter, mouse pad, and pencil cup (actually a recycled tin can!) look anything but ordinary when they're covered with the same leathers. This simple project involves cutting, decorative punching, and gluing.

SUPPLIES

Leather:

Gold velvet suede, 22" x 24"

Brown velvet suede, 14" x 20"

Leather lacing, gold or contrasting color

Optional: Extra leather or felt (19" x 11") to cover back of desk pad.

Other Supplies:

Papier mache desk pad, 19" x 12"

Foam mouse pad, 8-3/4"

Soup can, 4-1/2" x 3"

Leather cement

TOOLS

Cutting mat

Straight edge

Rotary cutter with straight and decorative blades

1/16" round punch (hand or drive)

1/8" diamond punch (hand or drive) (If using drive, you will need a mallet.)

Craft knife

Measuring tape

Clothespins

Old credit card or piece of mat board the same size

Patterns can be found on page 90.

INSTRUCTIONS

Cut:

1. Place cutting mat on work surface. Using the straight blade in the rotary cutter, cut two pieces gold suede, one 22" x 14" and one 9-1/2" x 5".
2. Cut two 3" squares from gold suede, then cut squares in half diagonally.
3. Place can on gold suede. Trace around bottom and cut out a round of gold suede, cutting inside the traced line.
4. Place decorative blade in cutter. Cut three pieces from brown suede, one 5" x 14", one 9-1/2" x 2-1/2", and one 8-1/2" square.

Punch:

1. Copy punch patterns on paper. Punch out designs on paper pattern.
2. Place a chalk mark in center of 5" x 14" brown suede pieces. Place pattern A on chalk mark 1/4" in from edge. Rub chalk over pattern to transfer design to leather. Repeat across both pieces, measuring 2" between center round punches.
3. Transfer pattern B to 9-1/2" leather, using above method and placing center rounds 2-1/4" apart.
4. Punch patterns in leather using hand punches or drive punches.
5. Punch one round between each pattern B.

Assemble Mouse Pad:

1. Spread leather cement across the top of the mousepad, using an old credit

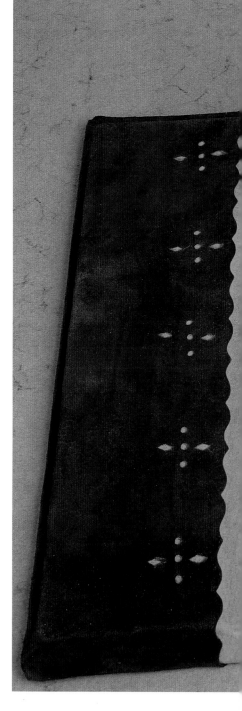

card. Center brown suede square over mouse pad and smooth into place, working from the center outward.
2. Spread leather cement over backs of gold triangles and place them in each corner. Allow to dry completely.

3. Trim off edges using a craft knife.

Assemble Blotter:

1. Spread leather cement over top of desk pad. Center large gold suede piece on pad and smooth into place, working from the center out to the edges. Firmly press leather into any grooves or depressions.

2. Turn over the desk pad and apply leather cement 1" wide all the way around the edges. Pull and smooth leather to back, folding and trimming at corners.

3. Apply cement to 14" punched brown suede pieces, keeping cement away from punched areas.

Continued on next page

continued from page 89

4. Position on sides of blotter, centering punched designs. Smooth into place, allowing 1" of leather to hang over edges.

5. Turn over blotter. Apply leather cement 1" wide all the way around the edges. Pull leather around to back and smooth, folding and trimming at corners.

6. *Option:* Cement leather or felt to back of desk pad.

Assemble Pencil Cup:

1. Cement the 9-1/2" x 5" gold suede

piece around the can. Allow excess to hang off the bottom edge.

2. Clip leather every 1/4" around bottom edge. Fold and cement leather to the bottom of the can.

3. Cement gold suede round to bottom of can.

4. Wrap and cement 9-1/2" long punched strip around can.

5. Wrap a piece of leather lacing around top edge of can. Cut to fit, butting ends. Glue to top, covering top edge of leather. ❏

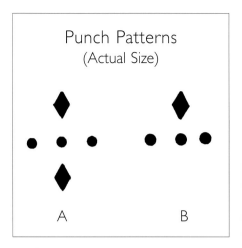

Punch Patterns
(Actual Size)

A   B

PORTFOLIO COVER

By Barbara Matthiessen

Dramatic diamond cutouts and silver corner covers decorate a red suede portfolio cover you make from a single piece of red suede. Cutting and gluing are all that's involved.

SUPPLIES

Leather:
Red suede, 18" x 21"
Black leather, 4" square

Other Supplies:
4 silver corner covers
Leather cement
1" square of hook and loop tape

Patterns can be found on page 92.

TOOLS

Cutting mat
Straight edge
Rotary cutter with straight blade
Scissors
Old credit card or mat board cut to same size to spread cement
Hammer
Heavy weights (e.g., books)
White chalk

INSTRUCTIONS

Construct:

1. Enlarge pattern as directed. Place pattern on wrong side of leather and trace around outline. Use scissors to cut out.

2. Fold up bottom flaps. Spread cement 3/4" wide along top and side edges.

Fold in top, then side edges, securing sides of bottom flaps. Place weights on edges and allow cement to cure.

Decorate:

1. Place cutting mat on work surface. Use rotary cutter and straight edge to cut

trim pieces:

From black leather, cut one 3" square and two 1-1/2" squares.

From red suede, cut one 1-1/2" square and one 5 1/4" x 1" strip.

2. Spread cement on all leather squares. Press on front of portfolio, using photo as a guide for placement. Place weights on squares while cement cures.

3. Diagonally trim one end of red suede strip to form a point.

4. Adhere hook and loop tape to trimmed end, trimming hook and loop tape as needed. Adhere other side of hook and loop tape to portfolio front 2" from edge.

5. Wrap strip around portfolio to back, allowing some slack. Cement other end of strip to the back of the portfolio.

6. Slide metal corners over leather corners. Hammer into place from inside. ❏

Pattern for Portfolio Cover

Enlarge @ 250% for actual size.

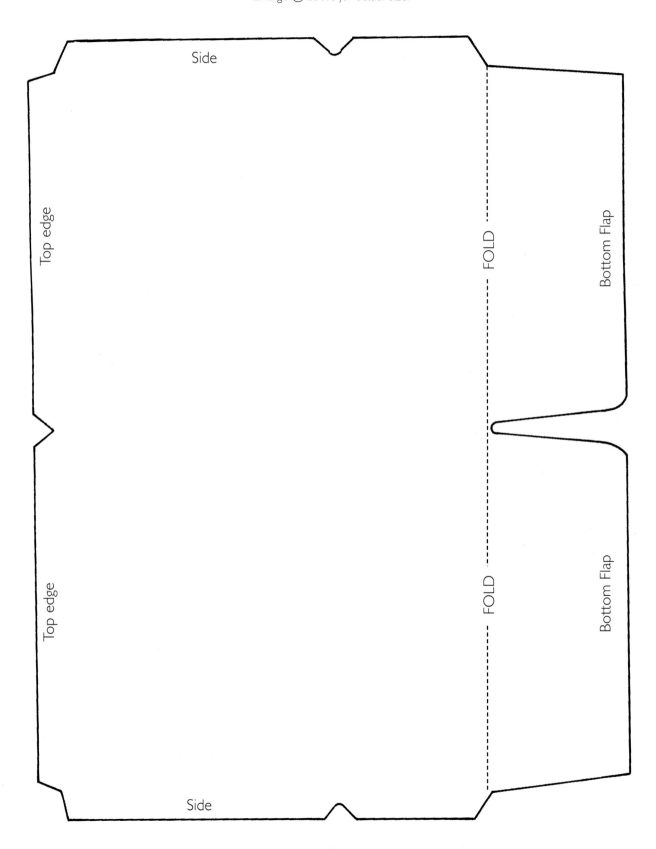

Pattern for Branded Book Cover & Bookmark
(Actual Size)

See pages 94 - 95 for instructions and photo.

BRANDED BOOK COVER & BOOKMARK

By Barbara Matthiessen

Simple designs, created with a woodburning tool on sturdy leather, decorate a book cover that is sized to fit a paperback book and a matching bookmark. Remember that leather burns quickly, so keep the tool moving as you burn the design.

SUPPLIES

Leather:

2 tooling leather sheets, 8-1/2" x 11"

Purple velvet suede, 6-1/4" x 3-1/4"

6 yds. natural kangaroo lace

Other Supplies:

Leather cement

4 brass brads, 3/16"

TOOLS

Utility knife

Cutting mat

Straight edge

1/8" round punch

Hammer

Measuring tape

Transfer paper

Pencil

Woodburning tool with round tip

Clothespins

Edge beveler

INSTRUCTIONS

Cut:

1. Place cutting mat on work surface. Using a knife and straight edge, cut the following pieces from one of the leather sheets:
   One 7" x 2" (for the bookmark)
   One 5-1/4" x 2-1/4" (for the book cover decoration)
   Two 3" x 8-1/2" (for the book cover ends)
   Reserve the other tooling leather sheet to make the book cover.
2. Diagonally trim off two adjacent corners on one end of the 7" x 2" bookmark piece.
3. Use the edge beveler to finish the edges of the bookmark.
4. Diagonally trim off all corners on the purple suede piece, cutting 1" from the corners on all sides.

Burn Design:

1. Transfer the patterns to the 7" x 2" bookmark and the 5-1/4" x 2-1/4" cover decoration piece by placing transfer paper on leather then center patterns on top. Trace over design lines with a pencil.
2. Heat woodburning tool according to the manufacturer's instructions. Use the tool to burn the designs on the leather pieces.

Make Book Cover:

1. Turn over reserved leather piece so the back side is facing up. Place 3" x 8-1/2" pieces on ends. Hold in place with clothespins.
2. Make a pencil mark every 1/2" all the way around the book cover.
3. Punch a hole at every mark 1/4" in from the edge. Punch one hole at the top of the book mark.
4. Using kangaroo lace, whipstitch the lace around cover. Start at one bottom edge, leaving a 4" tail. Lace two stitches in every corner. Tie off lacing securely.

Finish:

1. Cut lengths of lacing and attach to bookmark through the punched hole, using a lark's head knot.
2. Spread cement over colored suede. Smooth into place on front of book cover.
3. Cement woodburned cover decoration at center of suede.
4. Use a knife tip to poke holes in the corners for brads. Insert brads. Spread and flatten tips on the inside of the book cover. ❏

SUPPLIES

Leather:

Black upholstery leather, 5-1/2" x 5-1/2"

3/4 yd. black latigo leather lace

Other Supplies:

Leather finish

Black awl thread

3/8" brass grommet

Stencil with squiggles and spirals motifs

Textile medium

Acrylic craft paints - Black, metallic russet, metallic olive, metallic sunset gold

Poster board

Medium weight double polished clear vinyl, 2-1/2" x 5-1/2"

White glue

Contact cement

TOOLS

1/4" stencil brush

Artist's paint brushes: 3/4" wash, #1 script liner

Fine tip marker

Leather shears

Craft knife

Straight edge

Binder clips

Scratch awl

Mini punch set with 3/32" (size 1) drive punch

3/8" drive punch

Poly cutting & punching board

Wooden mallet

Paper towel

Water container

Clothes iron and ironing board

3/8" grommet setter

Patterns can be found on page 98.

STENCILED LUGGAGE TAG

By Lisa Galvin

Here's a way to make your black suitcase easy to identify – add a colorful stenciled tag. The clear vinyl for the window is available in the fabric departments of crafts stores.

INSTRUCTIONS

Cut:

1. Photocopy (or trace) patterns with punch and cut guides. Adhere to poster board. Cut out with a craft knife and straight edge.
2. Use binder clips to hold patterns in place on leather. Cut out pieces.
3. Cut one piece of clear vinyl to match outer edges of tag.
4. Use scratch awl to punch stitching holes around outer borders of leather pieces. **Do not** punch grommet hole yet.
5. On one piece of leather, punch holes at top of flap, using 3/32" (size 1) punch.

6. Cut insert slit and flap, following pattern lines.

7. Cut insert slit in clear vinyl, using pattern as a guide.

Paint & Stencil:

1. Paint front of tag with metallic olive, using a 3/4" wash brush.

2. Blend a small amount of black with the metallic olive for a deeper hue. Add a second coat of paint. Let dry.

3. Mix equal amounts textile medium and black paint. Position stencil on tag. Load stencil brush and gently dab off excess. Using a pouncing motion, stencil the spirals.

4. Stencil other motifs with metallic colors, using the photo as a guide.

5. Use a script liner to add highlight lines in contrasting colors.

6. Apply a small amount of sunset gold paint to stencil brush. Lightly pounce tag, adding highlights over stenciled designs and around outer edges. Let dry.

Assemble:

1. With back sides together, stack front and back pieces. Insert vinyl piece between the layers.

2. Thread needle with awl thread. Beginning at top of tag, bring needle through center hole on back of front piece, leaving a 4" tail extending to tie off later. Use a running stitch all the way around the outer border. Tie a knot between the layers at top when you are finished.

3. Cement outer edges of tag together for a finished look.

4. Cement the leather edge to the vinyl window, leaving the flap free. Remove excess cement by rubbing with your fingers.

5. Use a binder clip to clip the pattern to the tag. Punch the grommet hole through all layers.

6. Use grommet setter and mallet to insert grommet.

7. Spray tag, front and back, with leather finish. Let dry.

8. Fold latigo lace in half, bringing ends together and leaving a loop on one end. Slip ends through grommet, then through looped end of lace. Pull to attach at top of tag. Attach to luggage by threading one end of lace through handle and knotting ends together. ❑

Pattens for Stenciled Luggage Tag
(Actual Size)

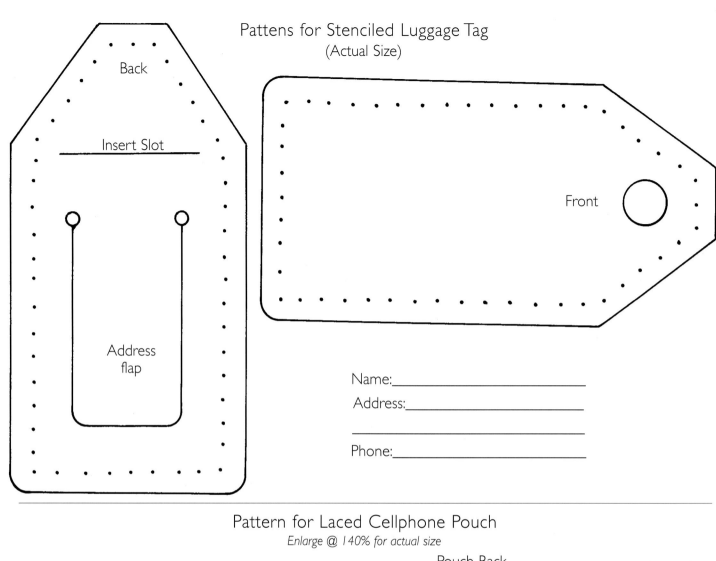

Back

Insert Slot

Address flap

Front

Name:_____

Address:_____

_____

Phone:_____

Pattern for Laced Cellphone Pouch
Enlarge @ 140% for actual size

Pouch Back
Cut 1

Cut

Fold

Cut

Belt Loop

Pouch Front
Cut 1

LACED CELLPHONE POUCH

By Patty Cox

This whipstitched suede cellphone pouch has loops on back for attaching to a belt. Using a marker to create the design is a simple, effective way to add color and interest.

SUPPLIES

Leather:

Sueded cowhide

Leather lacing

Other Supplies:

Snap

Maroon fine tip permanent marker

Sewing thread

TOOLS

Tool for attaching snap

Stitching punch

2-prong lacing needle

Leather shears

Sewing machine with leather needle

Transfer paper

INSTRUCTIONS

Construct:

1. Cut pouch front and back, using patterns provided, or adjust pattern as needed to fit your size cell phone.
2. Fold over belt loops and machine stitch to pouch back.
3. Using a stitching punch, punch stitching holes on pouch sides, 1/4" from edge.
4. Thread 2-prong needle with leather lacing and whipstitch sides.
5. Position snap and set.

Decorate:

1. Transfer design, using pattern provided.
2. Draw design on front with maroon marker. ❑

BEADED & FRINGED CELLPHONE POUCH

By Patty Cox

Reminiscent of a Native American belt pouch, this one is sized for carrying a cellphone. It has loops on the back so you can wear it on your belt. The fringe, cut with a rotary cutter, can be trimmed to any length.

SUPPLIES

Leather:

Chamois

Other Supplies:

Snap

Seed beads - Turquoise, orange, pale yellow

Thread

TOOLS

Tool for setting snap

Beading needle

Rotary cutter

Straight edge

Sewing machine with leather needle

Transfer paper

Iron

INSTRUCTIONS

1. Cut pouch front and back and belt loops, using patterns provided, or adjust to fit your size cell phone.
2. Transfer zig-zag beading pattern to wrong side of pouch front.
3. Following the beading pattern, thread four seed beads (one orange, three turquoise) on beading needle for each diagonal line of zig-zag. Sew on beads according to pattern.
4. Add yellow beads along zig-zag design.
5. Set snap in position on pouch front and flap.
6. Working one at a time, make the belt loops. Fold each long edge to inside, overlapping 1/2". Press each strip with cool iron.
7. Using sewing machine, topstitch 1/8" from each edge.
8. Fold each strip into a loop. Stitch loops on pouch back.
9. Sew pouch back to front.
10. Cut fringe 1/8" wide, using a rotary cutter and a straight edge. ❑

Beading Pattern

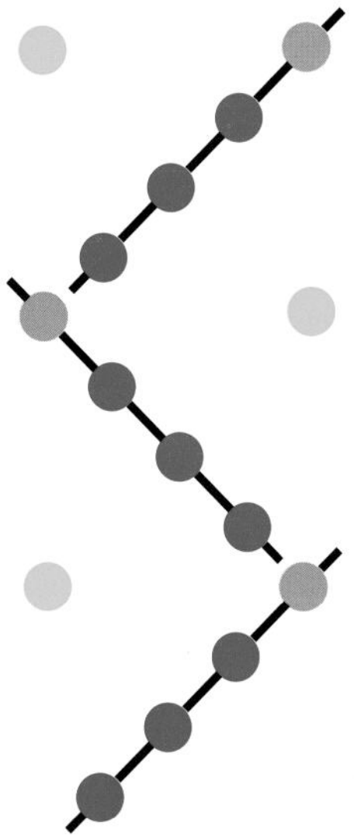

Pattern for Beaded &
Fringed Cellphone Pouch
(Actual Size)

Pouch Front
Cut 1

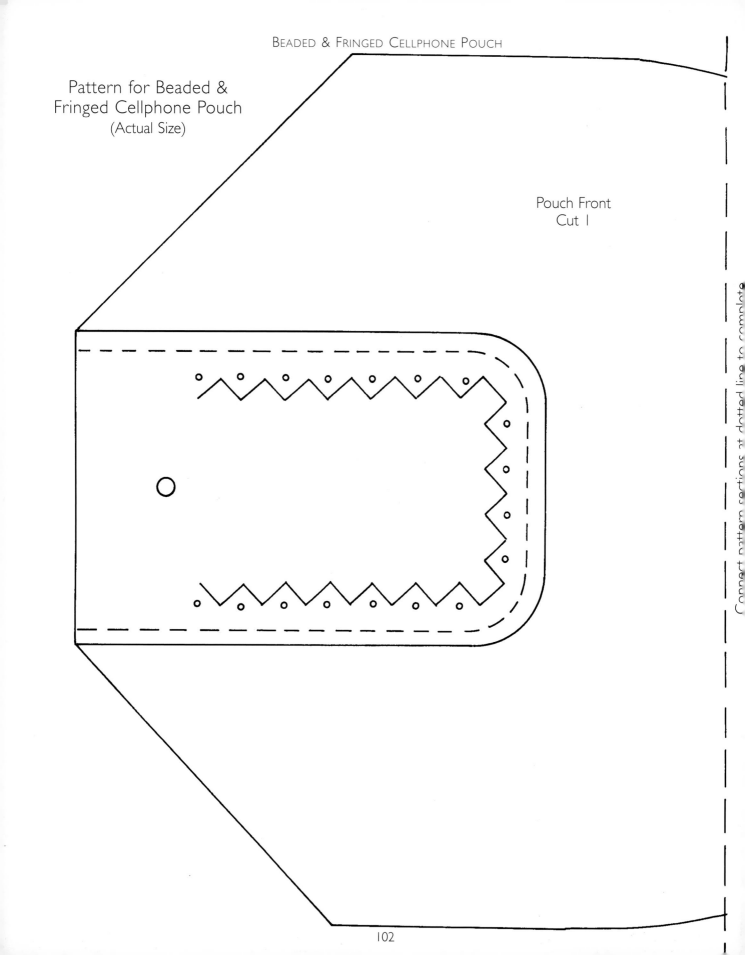

Connect pattern sections at dotted line to complete

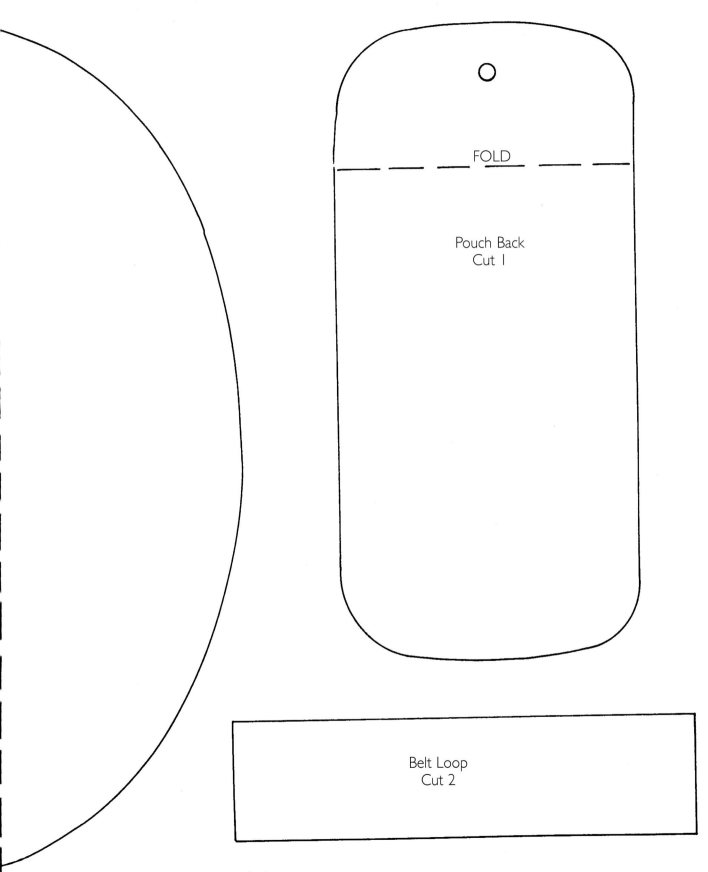

FOLD

Pouch Back
Cut 1

Belt Loop
Cut 2

SUPPLIES

Leather:

Thinnest vegetable tanned leather

Other Supplies:

Wire-bound photo album or journal with opening in front cover

Rubber stamp - Leaf motif

Permanent black ink pad

Ultra-fine point permanent black marker

Acrylic craft paint - Black

Spray leather sealer

Glue

Photocopy of photo

Paper

TOOLS

Craft knife

Metal ruler

Small paint brush

COVERED JOURNAL

By Jacqueline Lee

A rubber-stamped design on thin leather makes an attractive cover for a wire-bound notebook. Since the plastics used in many photo albums contain chemicals harmful to photos, I like to use photo corners and wire-bound blank books with acid free pages to display photos. Using photo corners gives the album pages a vintage look.

INSTRUCTIONS

1. Make a paper template of the front panel of your album.
2. Trace the template on the leather.
3. Cut out the leather piece, using a craft knife and a metal ruler.
4. Stamp the leaf on the leather in a random pattern, using permanent black ink.
5. Enhance the vein lines of the leaves with a permanent black marker.
6. Spray the leather with leather sealer. Allow to dry.
7. Paint all edges and the photo inset area of the front cover of the album with black paint.
8. Mark a 1/4" wide border on the three outside edges of the back cover (but not next to the wire binding) and the insides of the front and back covers.
9. Paint the 1/4" borders and the edges of the covers with black paint. Let dry.
10. Glue the stamped leather panel on the front.
11. Insert photo. ❏

SUPPLIES

Leather:

Ladies' leather vest

Acrylic Craft Paints:

Inca Gold (metallic)

Light Red Oxide

Maple Syrup

Raspberry Wine

Raw Umber

Turner's Yellow

Other Supplies:

White transfer paper

Outdoor acrylic sealer, satin sheen

Paint Brushes:

3/8" angled shader

10/0 liner

#4 round

INSTRUCTIONS

Prepare:

1. Mix equal amounts of each paint color with outdoor sealer.
2. Transfer design

Paint the Design:

1. Base all leaves with Turner's Yellow.
2. Float edges of leaves with *either* Raw Umber, Light Red Oxide, or Raspberry Wine, using the photo as a guide for color placement.
3. Paint all the vines with Inca Gold.
4. Paint the veins in the leaves and vines with Maple Syrup. ❑

Pattern for Painted Vines
Enlarge @ 130% for actual size.

AUTUMN LEAVES PAINTED VEST

By Karen Embry

Leather is a wonderful surface for painting. Here, a simple leaf and vines design brightens a vest in fall colors. You can embellish a vest you make yourself from leather scraps or buy a vest and paint it.

Section A
(see section B on page 108)
Connect pattern sections at dotted lines to complete.

Pattern for Autumn Leaves Painted Vest
Enlarge @ 130% for actual size.

Connect pattern sections at dotted line to complete.

Section B
(See section A on page 107)

Pattern for Imagination Painted Journal
(Actual Size)

See pages 110 and 111 for instructions and photo.

Imagination is more

important than Knowledge.

Karen Embry

Einstein

Imagination is more important than knowledge. Einstein.

Karen Embry

IMAGINATION PAINTED JOURNAL

By Karen Embry

A quotation from Albert Einstein adorns a purchased leather journal cover. The design is painted in vibrant hues of teal and violet.

SUPPLIES

Leather:

Leather journal cover, 9" x 6-1/2"

Acrylic Craft Paints:

Burnt Sienna

Dark Salmon

Georgia Peach

Orchid

Patina

Payne's Gray

Peach Cobbler

Teal

Terra Cotta

Violet Pansy

Artist's Paint Brushes:

Angled shaders - 1/4", 1/8"

Liner - 10/0

Rounds - #2, #5

Other Supplies:

Blue transfer paper

Acrylic outdoor sealer, satin sheen

INSTRUCTIONS

Prepare:

1. Transfer pattern to front of journal cover.
2. Mix equal amounts of each paint color and satin sealer.

Paint the Design:

Girl:

1. Paint face and neck with Georgia Peach.
2. Float bottom of chin with Peach Cobbler.
3. Base hair with Terra Cotta. Let dry. Float with Burnt Sienna.
4. Paint eyebrows with Terra Cotta.
5. Paint lips with Dark Salmon.
6. Paint eyelashes with Payne's Gray.
7. Paint line for nose with Peach Cobbler.

Stars:

1. Base stars to the right and left of girl's head with Patina.
2. Float these stars at bottom edges with Teal.
3. Base remaining stars with Orchid.
4. Float with Violet Pansy.

Lettering:

1. Paint the words "Imagination," "is," and "than" with Teal.
2. Paint the words "More," "important," and "knowledge" with Violet Pansy. Let dry.

Finish:

Apply one coat of satin sealer to painted areas *only*. ❑

HOLIDAY MEMORIES ALBUM

By Karen Embry

Painted gingerbread people are painted on the cover of a leather photo album.
Sealing only the painted areas keeps the good feeling of the leather cover but
protects the painted design.

SUPPLIES

Leather:
Photo album, 13" x 13"

Acrylic Craft Paints:
Ballet Pink
Burnt Sienna
Clay Bisque
Licorice
Magenta
Sterling Blue
Teddy Bear Brown
Wicker White

Artist's Paint Brushes:
3/8" angled shader
#12 flat shader
10/0 liner
1/4" deerfoot stippler

Other supplies:
Brush-on outdoor satin sealer
White transfer paper

INSTRUCTIONS

Prepare:
1. Mix each paint color with an equal amount of satin sealer.
2. Transfer the design

Paint the Design:
1. Paint lettering and stars with Clay Bisque.
2. Base gingerbread people with Teddy Bear Brown.
3. Float edges of gingerbread people with Burnt Sienna.
4. Paint curly linework around edges with Wicker White.
5. Paint mouths and eyes with Licorice.
6. Stipple cheeks with Ballet Pink. Let dry.
7. Stipple smaller area inside cheek areas with Magenta.
8. Paint noses with Burnt Sienna.
9. Stipple buttons with Wicker White. Let dry.
10. Then stipple smaller areas in centers of buttons with Sterling Blue.
11. Paint dots in centers of buttons with Licorice.
12. Paint gingerbread girl's lips with Magenta.

Finish:
Apply one coat of satin sealer to painted areas *only*. ❑

Pattern for Photo Album
Enlarge @ 160% for actual size.

NECK PURSES

By Barbara Mansfield

These charming neck purses are made from a single piece of leather – no sewing is required. The leather is embellished with paint and rubber stamps – you can cover the entire surface or just a few spots. Various embellishments at the center of the top flaps provide weight to hold the flaps in place and give a finished look.

SUPPLIES

Leather:

Light gray velvet suede trim,
3-1/2" x 9-1/2"

Other Supplies:

Rubber stamp - Bamboo motif

Black dye inkpad

Permanent fabric adhesive

Black cording with tassels

Silver button

2 jump rings

Black permanent ink pen

TOOLS

1/8" hole punch

Eyelets and eyelet setting tool

Hammer

Thin foam cushion to pad surface
for stamping

Bamboo Stamped Neck Purse

INSTRUCTIONS

Assemble:

1. Fold bottom of leather piece up 3-1/4". Glue sides close to edges.
2. Fold down top to overlap bottom and determine where eyelets should go (where the top folds). Punch holes and insert eyelets.

Stamp:

1. Ink the bamboo stamp thoroughly. Test on paper, reload, and stamp on suede, making sure to press the stamp evenly. *Tip:* It's best to stand up for this – you can put more pressure on the stamp that way, but be sure there's no ink on the edges of the stamp.
2. Touch up any spots that need more ink with the black pen.

Finish:

1. Place jump rings in holes at top. Place tasseled cord in the rings and close.
2. Glue silver button in center of top flap.

SUPPLIES

Leather:

Black velvet suede trim,
3-1/2" x 9-1/2"

Other Supplies:

Acrylic craft paint - Metallics and colors of your choice

Permanent fabric adhesive

Black cording with tassels

Rubber stamps - Motifs of your choice

Embellishments - Buttons, polymer clay, medallions, beads, tassels, etc.

TOOLS

1/8" hole punch

Eyelets and eyelet setting tool

Hammer

Old credit card cut into different shapes

Paper towels

Flat palette

Painted & Stamped Neck Purses

Two variations of this project are shown in the photo. These instructions are for making one neck purse.

INSTRUCTIONS

Paint & Stamp:

1. Squeeze paint colors on palette.
2. Dip credit card pieces in paint colors and pull across suede. Remember that the two ends of the suede are the parts that will show, not the middle. (That will be the back.) You can paint the whole surface or just a few areas – your choice. When you're satisfied with the look, let dry.
3. Stamp over paint with rubber stamps. Let dry.

Assemble:

1. Fold up bottom 3-1/4". Glue close to edges on both sides.
2. Fold down top. Determine where eyelets should be placed (where the top folds). Punch holes and insert eyelets.
3. Insert satin cording through eyelet holes and knot each side to secure.

Embellish:

1. Embellish the top flap at center – use a tassel with a button on top, a piece of polymer clay that has been pressed with a rubber stamp and baked, a lovely bead, or any embellishment you like. ❏

Pictured on opposite page, clockwise from top: Bamboo Stamped Neck Purse, Medallion Painted & Stamped Neck Purse, Painted & Stamped Neck Purse with Polymer Clay

TRAVEL TOTE

By Lisa Galvin

This handsome black tote is 15" wide and 29" tall — big enough to hold all your travel essentials or double as a stylish shopping tote.

SUPPLIES

Leather:

7 sq. ft. black upholstery leather

36" black two-strand braided leather trim

Other Supplies:

7 brass grommets, 3/8"

8 solid brass 1/4" Chicago screws

Leather finish

Black foam core poster board, 4-1/4" x 11-1/2"

Black nylon thread

Contact cement

Optional: 2 sheets poster board

TOOLS

Yardstick or measuring tape

Rotary cutter

Cutting mat

Straight edge ruler

Craft knife

Seam gauge

Sewing machine with size 18 needle

Iron and ironing board

Brayer

Dressmaker's pencil

Round hole drive punches, 1/4" and 3/8"

Poly cutting & punching board

Wooden mallet

3/8" grommet setter

Straight screwdriver

Leather shears

CUTTING TIPS

- For best results when cutting multiple pieces from leather, cut all pieces from poster board first. Because hide shapes vary, lay poster board pieces on leather to determine best layout for your hide.
- Binder clip pattern to leather before cutting out pieces using a rotary cutter and cutting mat.
- Always cut with grain side up and position patterns along the direction of backbone for less stretch.

Instructions follow on page 118.

continued from page 116

INSTRUCTIONS

Cut:

1. Using rotary cutter, cutting mat, and straight-edge ruler, measure and cut these pieces:

   One 14" x 32" (for bag portion of tote)

   One 4-1/4" x 32" (for top band)

   One 5" x 12" (for tote bottom)

   Two 3" x 38" (for straps) *Note:* For shorter straps, reduce the length but leave the width the same.

2. From remaining leather, cut one piece 4-1/4" x 11-1/2". Cement to top of foam core poster board. (This piece will be used to stabilize the bottom of the bag.) Set aside to dry.

Construct:

1. With right sides facing one another, binder clip 14" sides of bag piece together. Machine stitch 5/8" from edge, removing clips as you stitch. **Do not** backstitch.

2. To secure ends of thread, tie ends in square knots. Add a drop of cement to hold. Trim.

3. Press seam allowances flat to one side. Turn bag right side out and machine stitch 1/4" from seam line through all three layers of leather. Cement down remaining seam allowance on back. Use a brayer to press flat.

4. Place the 4-1/4" x 32" top band face down on a flat surface. Using a ruler, measure 2-1/4" from side edge. With dressmaker's pencil, draw a sewing guideline on back side of leather the length of the piece.

5. Place bag, right side facing up, under sewing machine foot. Beginning 3/8" past the center-stitched seam, slip top band behind bag with back side facing up. Align top edge of bag with sewing guideline marked on band. Machine stitch band to bag, stitching 1/4" from the bag's top edge, through the bag and band layers. Overlap the ends of the band as you return to the starting point. Leave 2-1/4" of band extending above bag. (**See Fig. 1.**) Knot thread ends to secure.

6. Cement band to body on back side. Fold down the 2-1/4" part of band (that extends above the bag) over the top of the bag along guideline. Cement. Roll with brayer to smooth.

7. Turn bag with wrong sides facing out. Lay on a flat surface with seam at center front. On back side of leather, mark center of opposite (seamless) side. Fold 5" x 12" tote bottom piece in half to find center. Mark center points of longest edges on back.

8. With right sides together, matching centers, binder clip bottom piece to bottom edge of bag, working your way around sides.

9. Machine stitch 1/4" from edge, easing corners and removing clips as you go along. Stitch a second line of stitching 3/8" from edge. Tie thread ends to secure and trim excess.

10. Press seams upward with iron, then cement to inside of bag. Use binder clips to hold until secure.

11. Cement foam core board, leather side up, inside tote bottom. Smooth bottom of bag against board and keep cemented bottom seams along outer edges of board.

Add Straps:

1. Measure, then press one long edge of each strap piece over 3/4", bringing wrong sides together. Fold remaining width to pressed fold line, laying 3/4" width so it overlaps the second folded section. Press each strap flat.

2. Machine stitch 1/4" from each side edge. (On edges with the 3/4" overlap, you will be stitching very close to raw edge of leather to secure.) Knot and trim threads at the ends.

3. Use drive punch, mallet, and punch-board to punch two 1/4" holes 3/4" apart at the end of each strap.

4. Punch corresponding holes in the top band of the tote about 3-1/2" to each side of center on both sides of bag through all three layers of the top band.

5. Attach straps to bag with Chicago screws, using screwdriver to tighten.

Finish:

1. Punch 3/8" holes approximately 7/8" from top edge along top band for grommets. Use grommet setter and mallet to insert grommets.

2. Apply cement to one end of braided trim to hold ends firmly together and prevent unraveling. Let set.

3. Beginning at stitched center seam, cement braided trim to tote bag, covering bottom edge of top band. Overlap at ends adding a little extra cement at overlap. Hold together until set. Trim excess braid. *Tip:* Excess cement can be easily removed by rubbing with your fingers or by making a small ball of dry cement and rubbing it over the area.

4. Spray with leather finish. ❑

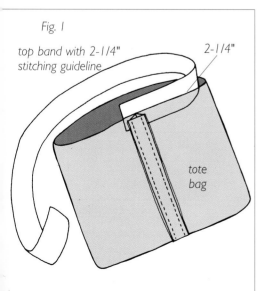

Fig. 1

top band with 2-1/4" stitching guideline

2-1/4"

tote bag

STAMPED PURSE

By Ann Mitchell of AnKara Designs

STAMPED PURSE

Pictured on page 113.

Two layers of leather are punched and stamped so one is visible beneath the other.
Leather tassels add weight to the top flap to help hold it in place. The following pages
include a photo of the back.

SUPPLIES

Leather:

Dark brown velvet suede, 18" x 24"

Red velvet suede, 18" x 24"

2 dark brown suede leather tassels, 4"

2 dark brown suede leather tassels, 2"

24 yds. kangaroo lace, 3/32"

Other Supplies:

Waxed brown thread

Rubber stamp - Medallion motif

Acrylic craft paint - Metallic bronze

Contact cement

TOOLS

2-prong lacing needle

Large eye needle

Scissors

White pencil

Pencil sharpener

Leather shears

Mallet

Poly punching board

3-prong lacing chisel, 1/8"

Diamond shaped leather punch

Round leather punch (size 5),
   11/64"

Large vinyl-coated paper clips

Cosmetic sponge wedge

Clear cellophane tape

Patterns can be found on page 126

INSTRUCTIONS

Cut:

1. Photocopy pattern pieces. Cut out.
2. Lay the pattern pieces over the brown velvet suede and trace around them with the white pencil. Using the leather shears cut out one each of the back and the front and two sides.
3. Lay the pattern pieces over the red velvet suede and again cut out a back, a front, and two side strips.

Punch Lacing Holes:

1. With the right sides facing up, lay one brown side strip over a red side strip and hold the pieces together with vinyl-coated paper clips. Repeat with the other two side strips.
2. With the right sides facing up, lay the brown front piece over the red front piece and hold together along the edges with paper clips.
3. With the right sides facing up, lay the red back piece over the brown back piece and hold together with paper clips.
4. Place one of the paper-clipped side strips on the punching board. Starting at the bottom, use the 3-prong chisel to make three lacing holes in the center of the strip 1/2" above the point and parallel to the sides. Next, place the chisel with one end prong in the punched hole farthest from the point at the bottom. Angle the chisel so it is parallel with the slope of one side of the strip, 1/8" from the edge. Punch the lacing holes. Repeat on the opposite edge, angling the chisel to follow the other edge. (The punched holes will form a V-shape.)
5. Continue punching lacing holes 1/8" from each side of the strip, spacing them by placing one chisel prong in the last

hole made. Make 52 holes on each side (this includes the three centered holes at the point.) Repeat for the second strip.

6. Lay the paper clipped front pieces of the purse on the poly punching board. Starting at the bottom point punch lacing holes into each side of the front pieces 1/8" from the edge using the same method of placing the chisel in the last hole of the previous punch. The bottom-most hole for each side should be the hole at the point of the purse front. Make 52 holes on each side. Use the chisel to punch 27 holes across the top edge of the front.
7. Lay the paper clipped back pieces of the purse on the punching board. Starting at the bottom point, punch lacing holes in each side of the back pieces 1/8" from the edge. (The bottom hole for each side is the hole at the point.) Make 52 holes on each side of the part that matches the front. Continue punching to the top point, making 26 holes on each side. (There should be a single hole at the top point.)

Stamp & Punch:

1. Separate the front pieces. Lay the brown front piece on a work surface. Use the cosmetic sponge to put a generous coat of paint on the rubber stamp. Center the design and stamp at the point of the pattern, being careful not to stamp over any lacing holes. Continue to stamp the purse front, using the photo as a guide.
2. Separate the back pieces. Lay the red piece on the work surface. Repeat the stamping process. Let dry.
3. With the cosmetic sponge, apply a generous amount of paint to the rubber stamp. Lay the stamp face up on a work

surface. Roll the top part of one of the tassels over the stamp, stamping the image all the way around the top of the tassel. Repeat with the other three tassels. Allow paint to dry.

4. Lay the brown front piece on the punching board. Use the diamond punch and the mallet to punch four diamond shapes from each stamped image. Repeat on the red back piece.

5. Punch the center of each stamped image, using the round punch.

Attach Tassels:

1. Lay the brown front piece back over the red front piece and paper clip in place, lining up the lacing holes. Lay the red back piece over the brown back piece and paper clip in place.

2. Spread a thin coat of contact cement on one side of the loop attached to one of the 4" tassels. Immediately lay it on the back side of the point of the red suede back piece. The loop should go around (not cover) the center lacing hole. Immediately pull the tassel back up. (This allows you to place the contact cement only where the loop is so that lacing holes are not cemented closed.) Reapply contact cement to the same side of the loop. Allow cement to set. Press loop on suede.

3. Apply a thin coat of cement to the side of the loop facing up. Press the brown suede of the back piece down on top of the loop and immediately peel back. Reapply contact cement to loop. Allow to set. Press brown suede back over the loop. (The tassel is now sandwiched between the two layers of the back piece.)

4. Repeat for the other three tassels, placing the other 4" tassel at the other end point of the back piece and the two 2" tassels at the smaller points. Allow to dry.

Lace:

1. Cut a 4 ft. piece of kangaroo lace. Fit the end of the lace in the 2-prong needle. Starting at the bottom of the purse, pull the lace from back to front of the front pieces through the hole at the point. Make one whipstitch around the right side of the purse to the next hole. On the next whipstitch, hold the wrong sides of the front piece and side strip together and attach the bottom hole of the side strip. Whipstitch up the side of the purse, stitching the edge of the front piece to the edge of the side strip. When you reach the top, turn the corner and whipstitch the top edge of the front piece. Pull the lace to the back when you reach the middle lacing hole and leave the excess.

2. Repeat on the left side of the purse, using a second 4 ft. piece of lace.

3. Cut two 3-1/2 ft. pieces of kangaroo lace. Turn over the bag and lace the edges of the back piece to the side strips. (The bottom three holes on each side strip are laced through twice, once on each side.) When you reach the top of the side strip, leave the remaining lace attached.

4. Cut two 2-1/2 ft. pieces of kangaroo lace. Starting at the center point at the top of the back, pull the lace through from back to front on the inside of the loop of the tassel and lace the edge of the back pattern together using a whipstitch. Leave the excess lace where it meets the lacing from the bottom half. Repeat on the other side.

5. Finish all the lace ends by putting the needle back on the end and pulling the lace through the whipstitches on the other side of the purse. At the top end with the tassel, pull the lace ends through the opposite stitches on the reverse side. At the bottom tassel, pull ends to the inside of the purse through the stitches on the inside. At the tops of the side strips, knot the two ends and pull the ends into the inside stitches down the sides of the purse. Trim and apply a dot of contact cement to fix in place.

Back of Purse

Finish:

1. Apply a thin coat of contact cement to the inside point of the back piece and a thin coat of contact cement to the inside point of the front. Allow cement to set. Press together, sealing the bottom point of the purse.

2. To make the strap, cut three 4 ft. pieces of kangaroo lace. Tape the ends together with clear tape and tape to your work table. Keeping the pieces flat with the right sides up, braid. Tape the second end. Trim ends, leaving 1/4" of tape.

3. Apply a thin layer of contact cement toward the back seam inside the two layers of the side strips. Apply a thin coat of contact cement to both sides of the bottom 1" of the braided lace. Allow to set. Place one end of the braided lace between the side strip layers and press to glue in place. Repeat for the other end, making sure the strap is not twisted.

4. Thread a large eye needle with a 6" piece of waxed thread. Run the thread through the topmost whipstitch on either side of one of the side strips. Pull the edges of the side strip together to form a pleat. Tie the two ends together. Dab a dot of clear nail polish on the knot for security. Repeat on the other side. ❑

SHOULDER STRAP PURSE

By Barbara Matthiessen

This box-style shoulder bag is handstitched with natural leather lacing. A sewing machine was used to stitch the straps.

SUPPLIES

Leather:

Gold suede, 20" x 36"

6 yds. natural leather lacing

Other Supplies:

1" wooden bead, 12mm

Sewing thread to match leather

Leather cement

TOOLS

Cutting mat

Straight edge

Rotary cutter with straight blade

1/16" round punch, hand or drive (If using drive, you need a mallet.)

Measuring tape

Clothespins

White chalk

Large-eye needle

Sewing machine with needle for sewing lightweight leather

Scissors

INSTRUCTIONS

Cut & Punch:

1. Place cutting mat on work surface. Cut these pieces from suede, using a rotary cutter and straight edge:
   One 10" x 24" (front, bottom, and back)
   One 3" x 24" (top lining)
   One 3" x 15" (tassel)
   Two 10-1/2" x 3" (side panels)
   Two 3" x 36" (straps)
2. Make chalk marks every 1/2" on all sides of front, bottom, and back pieces. Punch holes at every mark.
3. Use clothespins to attach side panels to front, bottom, and back pieces. (It will look like an open-ended box.) Use chalk to mark holes on side panel through holes punched on main piece.
4. Using a clothespin, pin the top lining piece, overlapping ends by 1". Mark with chalk. Unpin.
5. Punch holes on all panel and lining chalk marks.

Stitch & Make Tassel:

1. Using a clothes pin, pin side panels and lining to bag. Using lacing, whipstitch both side panels to main piece.
2. Cut 1/2" x 3" piece of tassel leather. Set aside. Cut fringe with scissors by cutting slits up to 1/4" from the other side, every 1/4".
3. Cut 12" of lacing. Apply cement along uncut 1/4" on fringed piece. Roll a couple inches, insert lacing ends, and roll up the rest. Apply cement to reserved 3" strip and press it along top of tassel. Run lacing through bead.
4. Clothes pin top of tassel lacing to center top of bag. Whipstitch lining to bag, catching the tassel in the lacing.

Make & Attach Straps:

Follow your sewing machine manufacturer's instructions for sewing lightweight leather, using the recommended needle and tension.

1. Fold strap pieces, right sides together, and sew, using a 1/4" seam allowance. Turn straps right sides out.
2. Punch two holes in the end of each strap. Punch 2 holes 2" down and 1" in from side seams of bag to attach each strap end.
3. Place strap ends inside bag. Run lacing through holes to outside of bag and knot ends to secure. ❏

BEADED HANDLE PURSE

By Barbara Matthiessen

This foldover handbag features cutouts of exotic leathers on the flap and a handle of beads strung on wire.

SUPPLIES

Leather:

Brown velvet suede, 14" x 10"

Scraps of exotic leathers

Other Supplies:

Leather cement

Your choice of glass beads (for handle)

Beading wire

Crimp beads

4 gold-tone eyelets, 1/8"

TOOLS

Measuring tape

Clothespins

Sewing machine and needle for sewing lightweight leather

Scissors

Eyelet setter

Wire cutters

Crimping tool

Old credit card or mat board cut to same size to spread cement

INSTRUCTIONS

Make Purse:

1. Lay out suede, wrong side up. Fold one 10" side in towards the center 5". Fold the other end in 3-3/4". (There will be a gap between the folds.) Use clothespins to hold for stitching.

2. Set sewing machine tension according to manufacturer's instructions for sewing lightweight leather. Starting at the lower right corner of the 5" fold, straight stitch up that side, across the fold on opposite end, and down the other side.

3. Insert two eyelets to each side in the gap between the folds, following the tool maker's instructions, placing the eyelet head on the right side of the leather.

4. Trim pieces of exotic leathers to random shapes and sizes. Arrange on bag flap. Spread cement evenly over the backs of leather pieces and smooth into place.

Make Beaded Handle:

1. Cut 40" of bead wire. Run wire through one set of eyelets. Pull ends even, then thread on crimp bead and crimp.

2. Thread beads on both wires for 14", then add a crimp bead.

3. Run wire ends through one eyelet of second set and out the other. Insert wires in crimp bead and through the holes in a couple more of the strung beads. Pull on wire to tighten beads. Crimp the crimp bead. Trim off excess wire. ❏

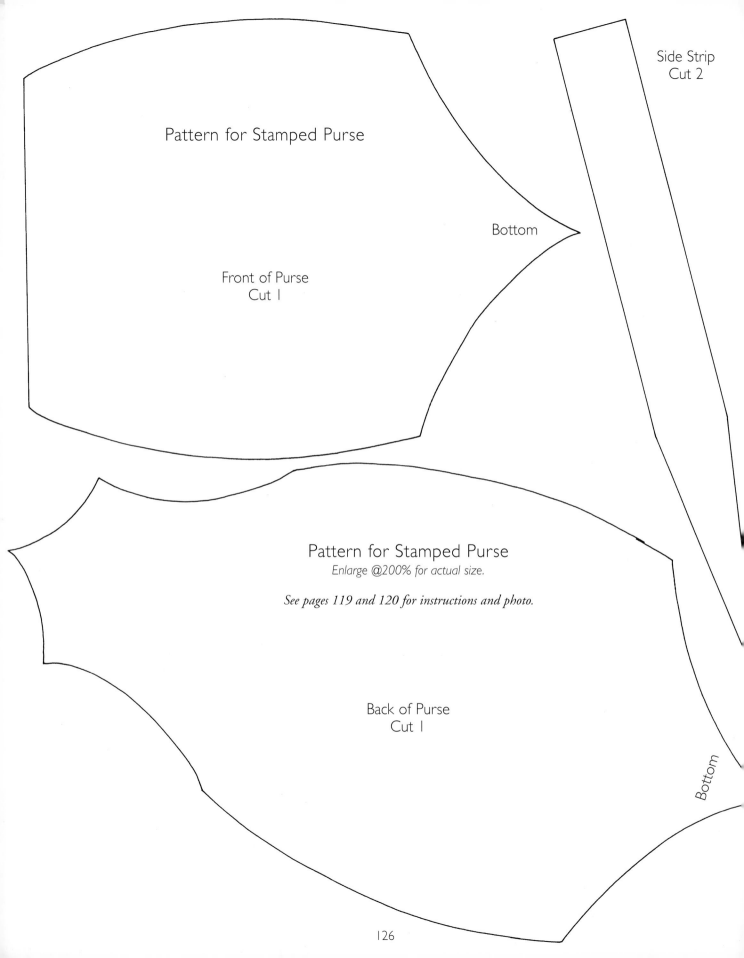

Pattern for Stamped Purse

Side Strip
Cut 2

Bottom

Front of Purse
Cut 1

Pattern for Stamped Purse

Enlarge @200% for actual size.

See pages 119 and 120 for instructions and photo.

Back of Purse
Cut 1

Bottom

METRIC CONVERSION CHART

Inches to Millimeters and Centimeters

Inches	MM	CM	Inches	MM	CM
1/8	3	.3	2	51	5.1
1/4	6	.6	3	76	7.6
3/8	10	1.0	4	102	10.2
1/2	13	1.3	5	127	12.7
5/8	16	1.6	6	152	15.2
3/4	19	1.9	7	178	17.8
7/8	22	2.2	8	203	20.3
1	25	2.5	9	229	22.9
1-1/4	32	3.2	10	254	25.4
1-1/2	38	3.8	11	279	27.9
1-3/4	44	4.4	12	305	30.5

Yards to Meters

Yards	Meters	Yards	Meters
1/8	.11	3	2.74
1/4	.23	4	3.66
3/8	.34	5	4.57
1/2	.46	6	5.49
5/8	.57	7	6.40
3/4	.69	8	7.32
7/8	.80	9	8.23
1	.91	10	9.14
2	1.83		

INDEX

Continued on next page

INDEX